Live Confident and Free

7 Powerful Steps for Living Your Best Life Happily, Authentically, and Unapologetically!

Erica Aker

Live Confident and Free

7 Powerful Steps for Living Your Best Life
Happily, Authentically, and Unapologetically!

Erica Aker

T&J Publishers

A SMALL INDEPENDENT PUBLISHER WITH A BIG VOICE

Printed in the United States of America by
T&J Publishers (Atlanta, GA.)
www.TandJPublishers.com

© Copyright 2022 by Erica Aker

All rights reserved. This book or parts thereof may not be reproduced in any form, stored in a retrieval system, or transmitted in any form by any means-electronic, mechanical, photocopy, recording, or otherwise-without prior written permission of the author, except as provided by United States of America copyright law.

Cover Design by Timothy Flemming, Jr. (T&J Publishers)
Book Format/Layout by Timothy Flemming, Jr. (T&J Publishers)

ISBN: 9798218004088

To contact author, go to:
Website: www.confidentandfree.com
Email: erica@confidentandfree.com
www.facebook.com/erica.hugheyaker
www.facebook.com/confidentandfree
www.instagram.com/EricaAker
www.instagram.com/_confidentandfree
www.youtube.com/confidentandfree
www.linkedin.com/in/EricaAker/
www.pinterest.com/EricaAker
Twitter: @EricaAker

This book is dedicated to my late sister, Audrey A. Hughey Duncan; my church sister, Cynthia Perry; and my uncle, Leroy "Peacemaker" Jackson. Their deaths were the catalysts that triggered the life-changing events shared in this book. The trauma of these deaths will always be etched in my mind. Although extremely painful, my life would not be what it is today had I not gone through those experiences

ACKNOWLEDGMENTS

I realize that each and every person that has crossed my path was for divine purpose. Our encounter may have been good, bad, short-term, or long-term, but the purpose was fulfilled. Had I not gone through the different experiences that had a hand in shaping and molding me, I would not have been able to grow into the woman I was destined to be at this appointed time.

To the friends who allowed me to vent and cry, you who listened and encouraged me in my life and to write this book. Thank you and I will forever be grateful to you for being 100% real with me when I wanted to wallow in my comfort zone instead of walking in my full potential.

Thank you for the rebukes, corrective criticism, and even a few cuss words that needed to be spoken when necessary, to snap me out of self-pity and wanting to remain a victim. Y'all know who you are and know that you are truly appreciated.

I want to thank myself for learning about the importance of self-love, self-care, and forgiveness. I am thankful for implementing various actions to dig myself out of depression without the use of medication. I am thankful that God kept me and gave me a sane mind to acknowledge and heal unhealed areas of my life.

Lastly, thank you, God! The giver of life. Thank you for entrusting this life to me, for loving and forgiving me when I was less than pleasing in your sight. Thank you for imparting wisdom to search and listen within so I could live unapologetically and strive to be the best person I can be. I will continue to learn and grow as you open my eyes to see beyond the surface on deeper levels.

Table of Contents

FOREWORD	xi
PREFACE	xiii
INTRODUCTION	15
1 DECIDE	29
2 SURRENDER	49
3 VISUALIZE	67
4 IGNITE	71
5 CONQUER	79
6 OVERCOME	111
7 EMBRACE	113
BONUS CELEBRATE THE NEW YOU	123

FOREWORD

I have known Erica and her family for over 30 years, practically all of my life. She and I grew up in the same area.

Within the last 7 to 10 years, some of her social media posts caught my attention. Many of her posts make readers stop, think, and evaluate themselves.

After inquiring about some of the messages, Erica afforded me the privilege and opportunity to read her book Confident and Free.

As a stylist for many years, she has helped several women by turning her chair into a couch. As she spent time listening and advising people, this book could also help you, but it's only for those who desire to change.

Confident and Free is a book written to help readers come out of bondage, be true to themselves, not be bound by the past or by the opinions of others.

Within this book, we may begin to ask ourselves if we have an authentic relationship with God that is true or do we stand on rituals and religion. In addition, Confident and Free helped me prepare devotionals and some of my sermons.

Erica stands on Godly principles and what the word says regardless of what society and the world accepts.

I believe this book could be helpful to anyone who has an open mind to hear her message of living life Confident and Free.

—Christopher Alexander Wimberly
Pastor of Hunter Hill First Baptist Church

PREFACE

As a child, I always knew that I was different. I did not fit in with any crowd and although I had a set of friends that I spent most of my time with, I was still a loner in many ways. I never had a high interest in most things middle and high school girls enjoyed, you know, gossip, boys, fashion, and giggling over silly things.

My favorite pastime was being a thinker. Anything deep that challenged my mind intellectually captured my interests. For most, this would be boring, right? Interestingly, my thoughts were very broad for a kid in high school. At the time, one of my favorite things to do was solve riddles. This challenged me to think on a deeper level.

As a result, this spilled into my daily life. I developed a keen level of awareness. I observed things that most of my peers either ignored or did not pick up on. I believe it started at this point in my life when my intuition, instincts, and discernment began to grow.

I went on to college, beauty school and dove into my career as a hairstylist. I enjoyed a successful career in the beauty industry, but deep down, I felt there was more for me to do. I dibbled and dabbled in various areas of the beauty industry but there was nothing that was quite as satisfying as my love for hair… until I launched into coaching, educating, and inspiring.

I created a business coaching and educating beauty professionals on how to create a successful beauty business for themselves. I participated in major hair shows as an educator. I authored several digital e-books, as well as, my first hard copy book that followed.

As time went on, my interest in the beauty industry began to fade. I still loved coaching and educating, but I felt a tug within saying it was time to go to another level. After a 3 year off and on battle with depression after my sister Audrey passed, I began to live my life like it was my last day.

This spurred me to launch Confident and Free. I help women and a few smart men, to live their best life TODAY, authentically, unapologetically, and fulfill their purpose and destiny with more confidence and freedom.

INTRODUCTION

Life Forever Changed

The room was quiet with a few family members chatting while sitting around the hospital bed… waiting. It was not cold, as some hospital rooms tend to be. It was eerily peaceful. I was holding her hand, my brother was beside me talking to her. She seemed to have waited patiently all day for him to get there as he traveled from Missouri to Georgia. Although she was unconscious, I believe she was very aware that we were all there.

We told her that we loved her and that she did not have to worry about Austin, her 16 year old son. We promised that we would look after him and that he would be taken care of.

As the day went on, her inhales and exhales grew slower and slower, with longer pauses in between each breath. I knew the inevitable was happening. She was literally dying in front of me but it all seemed so surreal.

Finally, after a few more long pauses in her breathing, she took her last breath. Her chest no longer moving up and down. Blood no longer flowing through her veins.

It was quite obvious, her life had departed her body. Only a lifeless shell remained.

It happened on Sunday November 13, 2016 at 4:10 p.m. Audrey, my sister, my friend, my inspiration, was gone. It was a day that I will never forget because. It was the day that changed my life forever.

They say that death can do that to you. It was true for me. On that day, a part of me died also. Life as I knew it, was and has never been the same again.

THE JOURNEY JUST GOT REAL

About a year after Audrey's death, I experienced what some call, The Dark Night of the Soul (a form of spiritual depression) that triggers a major Spiritual Awakening. This awakening is a life changing experience in which one's life has been shaken in such a way where enlightenment occurs. This phenomenon has been linked to external life events or disasters that may trigger this deep and profound change in a person's life. Events such as a tragic death of a loved one, an interruption of your perceived idea for your life's meaning, or any other event that could be considered a disaster.

The person that is experiencing the Dark Night of the Soul is experiencing the process of one's "old self" dying in order for the "new self" to emerge. Not a literal death, but a death of the egoic sense of self. This process is extremely painful, emotionally, mentally, and spiritually. In some cases, physical pain occurs as well.

One thing that I can say based on my experience of going through this is, no one truly understands this event unless they have actually experienced it. If they have actually trudged through the long journey of being refined in met-

INTRODUCTION

aphorical fire, burning away former beliefs, ideas, and way of life as they have always known it. Ironically, it is not a process one chooses to go through, it just happens.

Believe me, had it been a personal choice, I would not have willingly gone on this journey. I had grown quite content with my former life as it was.

There was not much help that I could get from friends, family, professional or Christian council. I never felt comfortable enough to share this unique experience and when I did I was always met with blank stares. I only had one friend that I could talk to, who somewhat understood. This was because her mother had had a very similar experience as mine. Neither her family, friends, nor Christian advisors could give her any reasonable help either.

What truly helped me navigate through this dark time in my life, was a small community of people that I found online that shared almost identical stories as mine. This helped me tremendously and they reassured me that what I was experiencing was not because I was mentally ill or crazy.

As I looked back on my past, there were many major events that happened in my life that jump started this journey. I can now see that it started well before 2016. There were so many things that happened in my life that played a significant role in my journey today.

A few major events that come to mind include: becoming sick with Leukemia at age 11, failing in college, failed friendships, failed relationships and failed business ventures. Besides my sister Audrey, I was also physically present during the transitional death of an uncle, and even one of my parent's pet dogs.

Don't get me wrong, I have had a lot of good things to happen in my life, but life was still very hard for me. Bad things "seemingly" outweighed any good that might have happened. Oftentimes, I questioned "why do I have to suffer so much? Why do I have to work twice as hard to achieve success?" I could not understand what I was doing wrong.

I went to church, I prayed, quoted scriptures, and had full faith in believing those scriptures. I sought out mentors, and lived my life as righteously as I possibly could. I had always been told this was the right way to operate in faith. It seemed God either left me or enjoyed ignoring my prayers. It certainly did not look like the life that God was giving others who were not anywhere near following his word as closely as I was trying to.

Over the years this took a toll on my self-esteem, self-worth, hope, and faith. I began to believe I was simply destined to live a life of hurt from disappointment, pain, abandonment, rejection and failure.

Over time, I later discovered that I was not a failure, but I had literally created a reality of failures sub-consciously out of my fear of failure. By not believing in myself, and thinking that I did not deserve the good of the land I saw others getting, I was unconsciously self-sabotaging any success for my life by believing the lies that my mind told me. Lies such as, "You're not good enough. You are from a small town, why would anyone listen to you? You don't have many friends. You don't have a degree." And the list went on and on, of the things that I would criticize myself on.

I did not realize that I was destroying myself all along. My focus stayed on all of the negative narratives in my life. I was attracting bad outcomes because of my negative inner

INTRODUCTION

voice.

Throughout the years, I have almost 30 years under my belt in the beauty industry as a hairstylist. I have encountered a multitude of women who have unknowingly, followed this same destructive pattern of behavior.

Which brings me to the tone of this book. It focuses not only on my personal experiences, but I am writing for women and a few men that are not living the best version of themselves because of un-beliefs created in their mind.

I have taken the baton to be the voice of many who feel unworthy, unheard, and those that are unhealed.

Lives are not being lived authentically. Either they are controlled by what others might think, what society has taught, or the ultimate destroyer, FEAR. My intention is to invoke a change in thought to that behavior and belief. My purpose is to encourage everyone to stand tall and live everyday like it's your last, walking confident and free.

My sister Audrey's death inspired me to live my life confident and free as authentically and unapologetically as I possibly can. My goal is to help others to do the same.

THE BACK STORY: HOW DEATH CHANGED ME
Audrey, a single mom, died from a debilitating and very rare autoimmune disorder called Mixed Connective Tissue Disease. She fought hard for many years and had multiple near death experiences. When she succumbed to this illness she left behind her 16 year old son and… me.

Although I fully accepted her death, I still took it really, really, really hard. But, in my heart, I would rather see her gone than to watch her suffer with zero quality of life. Nevertheless, her death still tore me up.

LIVE CONFIDENT AND FREE

In October 2017, Eleven months after Audrey passed, my church sister Cynthia, died from a long battle with cancer. She left behind a husband and seven children. Many of us were fervently praying and believing God for her healing also. That did not happen. It felt as if I was reliving my sister's death all over again. My tears had not stopped flowing for Audrey and now there were even more tears after Cynthia died.

Three months later after Cynthia passed, it was a cold, icy day in January 2018. I was talking to my mom on the phone. She was letting me know that once the snow and ice melted a bit, she was going to go check on her brother "Peacemaker" (as he we affectionately called him), his real name was Leroy.

It was barely thirty minutes after I had hung up, that mom called me right back. This time, she was screaming, hollering and crying. I had no idea what had happened so quickly that had her carrying on in such a way. Through her shaky voice and tears, she informed me that my uncle's home was on fire and that he was still inside.

As she waited anxiously for firefighters to get the flames under control, she continued to wail in grief. Mom, my aunt and my dad were helplessly standing on the sidelines of the street, watching the flames engulf and consume the house. It was unbearable to watch, I'm sure. When the firemen finally got the flames under control, in the words of emergency personnel, "it was no longer considered a rescue for a life. It was now considered a recovery for a body". Uncle Peacemaker was found dead very close to the front door, as if he was attempting to get out.

My mother's screams ripped my soul out. All I could

INTRODUCTION

do was stand frozen, in shock, holding the phone to my ear trying desperately to process what I just heard. Soon after, my mom had to hang up with me to talk with the authorities.

As for me, the shock began to wear off and reality began to sink in. I lost all control and went into a fit of my own screams and loud wailing. I was helpless. I couldn't get to my family and be there as a support. The driving conditions from the weather was too bad to be on the roads. They were icy and frozen. I could not leave my home at all.

My mind kept replaying my mom's screams over and over. Visions of Peacemaker trapped in his home, doused in flames, trying to get out, consumed my thoughts. All of these events overwhelmed me tremendously. Days later after the fire, my face broke out into hives. My face was inflamed and my eyes were literally swollen shut as if I had been stung by a swarm of bees. Initially, I thought I was having an allergic reaction, but I later realized my body was reacting to severe stress in the form of hives and swelling.

After each of these traumatic events, I went through two years of depression from 2017-2019 off and on continuously. I was sad, devastated, shocked and angry with everything and everybody, including God. Strangely, in the midst of all the chaos, I began to experience a form of enlightenment or epiphany's, as some call it.

My eyes seemed to open. Things became brighter and clearer. Not physically, but more so in a spiritual way. I could see things beyond what my physical eyes could see or understand. My vision became very clear and I was aware of everything and every person around me. I could see clearly through lies, fake behavior, and manipulation. I saw past exterior surface levels and could see vividly on deeper levels.

I've always been observant and discerning, but this was different. My level of awareness was being refined and sharpened on a deeper spiritual level.

Have you ever seen the movies, The Matrix, Lucy, or Limitless? This would be the best way that I could describe my experience of seeing what everyone else did not. In all three movies the character's eyes were opened to see things in an extraordinarily heightened way. The only difference with me was, my awareness was not provoked by taking a pill, as in these movies.

I could see a person's true intentions if they were being real or fake. I could read past what they were verbally saying and could easily discern what they were not saying. I can honestly say, I've always had the ability to read people just by watching them, but this was on another level of any type of spiritual gift that I had ever been given in the discernment genre.

I began to question everything about life in general and also about my own life. The Characteristics of "life" became my focus. Life as I knew it, had no more meaning to me. There had to be more to life than what I had previously experienced. I saw how I had settled in many areas of my life where I was not living up to my full potential. My purpose and destiny were not being fulfilled.

Thus, the spiritual quest began.

After my journey started, it began to challenge me in major ways to be more open, more real, and more authentic. I desired to live a life where I was fully confident in myself and free to be whomever I was, without caring about any judgement or criticism coming from other people or society.

INTRODUCTION

Somewhere in life we have been taught to care about what other people think and worry about their thoughts or ideas concerning other humans' personal lives.

The questions I had, no one could seem to give me satisfying or factual answers. I soon realized that much of what I knew or had been taught were merely untruths, opinions or old wives tales that had been passed down from past generations. Mostly opinions not based on facts.

My spiritual journey began at this moment to seek truth or at least some type of understanding about this thing we call LIFE. I needed to shed thoughts and beliefs that had created strongholds in my life, such as, abandonment issues, rejection, low self-esteem, fear and doubt.

Now before anyone gets triggered by the word "spiritual", my personal spiritual journey has nothing to do with religious beliefs. Although some of my religious beliefs were impacted, Spiritual for me is, walking my own path to reasoning and understanding by asking questions and receiving answers that make logical sense to me or by what resonates with "me" from a spiritual plane of understanding. I distanced myself from all the noise and chatter and listened closely within. Meaning, I listened and looked for what felt right for me deep down inside.

It is not about an answer that sounds good or using a catchy Christian cliché when there is no definite answer. I'm not here to force, debate or debunk anyone's personal religious beliefs. We've all been given the power of choice and experience. What you choose to believe is your personal business. Your life experiences will likely be different from mine. So there is no reason for me to argue right vs wrong, religion vs spiritual, black vs white, democrat vs republican, or anything else where beliefs come into play.

As I stated before, these major events jump started my spiritual journey. I found so many answers to a lot of unanswered questions that resonated and made sense to me when I applied them to my life. This new way of thinking was very strange, yet liberating. I soon began to focus on living my life as full as I possibly could, with no regrets. I found myself not worrying any longer about what others thought about my truth. If it felt right in my intuitive gut, I no longer cared about someone else's opinion. As far as I am concerned, if there are no facts to base answers on, I consider them opinions, which I believe I am entitled to have my own also.

Before moving any further, I must put out this DISCLAIMER: *Everything written in this book is either based on facts or will include my personal opinion. I don't expect everyone to agree with me, but if you choose to do so, that is up to you. You have a right to your own personal beliefs and opinions.*

*Many of the stories or examples that I share are based on true events. However, some names and certain parts of the truth have been changed or rearranged in order to maintain the privacy of individuals involved.

This book is basically written as a guide for inspiration and encouragement, based on my own personal experiences. It is written to help those that seek to live a life that enables them to be Confident and Free. I recommend that you take from what is written, the ideas that resonate with your spirit and throw away what does not.

This book is not specifically a religious book for Christians or any other particular faith, but may contain some perspectives and references from the Bible and God (which I choose to believe

INTRODUCTION

in). I do not necessarily express my thoughts from a theological point of view but rather a psychological point of view.

Although this book is quick and easy to read, it needs to be digested. Why? Because change is a process. It does not happen overnight. Take your time expounding on the questions that are presented. As you read, take time outs to ask yourself what does your own intuition and gut tell you. By doing this, you can make more informed decisions that are best suited for yourself.

To be further clear regarding "my personal beliefs", I choose to be a part of the Christian community. I believe Jesus is the son of God and that he died so that I could have eternal life. However, there are some beliefs that I no longer believe that were taught over the years. Because I have received personal revelation on some of those teachings, I now view some of those former beliefs from a different perspective.

Many of my beliefs were passed down from other people, such as, family, teachers, preachers, television, authority figures, and friends. Many of those beliefs no longer resonate with my spirit within. It is not to say that I'm right and someone else is wrong. I'm merely stating, I may not believe or agree with every single piece of information that was passed on to me. I may disagree with someone else's personal beliefs that may not align with mine. However, I can absolutely guarantee that I will respect anyone's personal beliefs one hundred percent! I only ask that you respect mine as well.

Now that I've covered that, let's continue on with walking through life while embracing a lifestyle that will lead us to living more confident and free…

You may be asking, what does living confident and free mean exactly?

LIVE CONFIDENT AND FREE

Confident and Free was birthed out of the idea that many women in particular (like myself), and some men have become stagnant and complacent in their lives. One may feel there is no fulfillment in the day to day life. It may feel like you know there is more to your life than getting up day after day going to work, seeing about family, paying bills, traveling only once or twice a year, going to school, church, or doing something fun periodically. You might find yourself rinsing and repeating this same pattern year after year.

You know deep within your heart that something bigger is out there. You know that you have a greater purpose and destiny that is not being carried out. You are miserable and unhappy, but yet you manage to create a comfort zone that is safe within the box that life has "dealt" to you. You have accepted the belief that this is the life God must have meant for you to have.

There are actually those who believe that their current situation of being poor, miserable, unhappy, sick etc. is the life they must accept. Did you know "As a man thinks, so is he"? If you believe that, you will get exactly that. Think about that for a minute.

Other reasons you may not be living up to your full potential could be as follows:

- Fear of what others will think or say
- Procrastination (I will live my best life when the kids are grown, when I retire, when I get more money, etc.)
- Lack of faith and belief in self
- Past traumas causing you to be the victim (emotional, physical, spiritual)
- Fear centering around abandonment, rejection, and anx-

INTRODUCTION

iety, that cause self-sabotaging behaviors
- Low self-esteem, low self-worth (I'm not good enough, smart enough, pretty enough, etc.)
- Unsupportive environment
- Poverty and lack mindset or mentality

Confident and Free is about inspiring and encouraging women and a few smart men, to stand in their true authentic self. To become the best version of themselves without holding back or bringing judgement upon self. Confident and Free is about walking with your head held high for living in a way that brings joy, peace, happiness, success, good health and prosperity externally and within. Confident and Free focuses particularly on:

- Self-love
- Self-acceptance
- Adventure
- Travel
- Conquering goals, ideas, and dreams
- Finding your true purpose and walking into your destiny
- Healthy living
- Money and wealth
- Better relationships
- …and whatever else you have always wanted, but held back because of fear of judgement, or ridicule, not only from others, but also from that critical inner voice within your own head.

LIVE CONFIDENT AND FREE

1

Decide

BE CONFIDENT AND FREE BY ASKING YOURSELF: ARE YOU HAPPY?

This is a question many answer slowly by saying, yes, but when asked, "Why are you happy?" they are not able to explain why they are happy. Then I will switch the question to, "do you want to be happy?" I noticed when the question is asked in this order, I will quickly get a yes for the answer. Why are so many people walking in uncertainty?

I remember on many days constantly saying to myself, "I just want to be happy" over and over again. I often wondered how my unhappy life could somehow switch into being full of happiness. The more I said, "I just want to be happy," the more I felt unhappy.

Why was life being so cruel? Why couldn't I be happy every day? Sure, I found temporary happiness with various material things, activities and certain people that I enjoyed, but that happiness only lasted as long as I was directly involved with it. Once the moment or day was over, I was right back where I started from.

I even googled how to be happy. I read that happiness is found within. Well, if this were true, why wasn't mine showing up?

As I began to think more deeply about happiness and what it means when it has been said "happiness comes from within". I have since discovered that, it wasn't that happiness was not there, I had to realize that happiness is a choice and that we have to tap into it from within.

As long as I continued to feel sorry for myself, maintain a negative perspective, and continue to believe the lie that I was not happy, I discovered that I manifested exactly what my thoughts focused on. My true inner conscious belief system was saying, "You are unhappy, stay unhappy".

This was nothing more than the obvious truth. I had embraced a victim mentality towards my own happiness and I had become very comfortable not working to change my situation. I was stroking my own ego. The bottom line was that happiness stayed away because subconsciously, I would sabotage my happiness by remaining a victim.

Let that marinate and soak in your spirit for a moment.

If I were to be honest, it felt good to my ego to blame everything and everybody for my sad life. The lack of love towards self was comfortable. I had to admit, I was at zero in the self-love department. What is the opposite of love? Hate. I finally had come to terms that I hated myself once I got REAL with the person I was looking back at in the mirror. Of course hate is a powerful word, but again, the opposite of love is hate and I certainly wasn't loving myself. I guess I could soften the verbiage by saying that I had a strong dislike for myself.

1   DECIDE

This was a painful wakeup call and realization in self-awareness. "Erica you don't love yourself, you hate yourself." Simple. I was attracting exactly what my energy was putting out.

Once I realized this revelation, I then had to figure out, where did the self-hatred come from? This process took a lot of time, effort, and intentional focus on going back, digging in my past, sitting with myself, and opening my heart in order for truth to come forth.

I went as far back as I could remember. The 4th or 5th grade stood out. I was best friends with a girl in my class. We had the best of friendship together. We played hopscotch, box ball, jumping rope, and the friendship was full of laughter. Then one day out of the blue, she moved away. We kept in touch, but over time our friendship shifted. We were no longer the elementary school buddies that we once had been. She developed friendships with other girls and had become closer to them. It was no longer just the two of us. How could that happen, I thought I showed just how loyal I could be as a friend?

With my introverted personality, which I understood much later in life, caused me to be awkward, I did not fit in well with girl groups. I was a loner, and perfectly happy with just one friend. My 10 year old mind didn't understand why everyone else did not see friendship this way also. We only needed one friend.

I really do not know how my young mind processed all of that, but as I began to think about this on my spiritual journey, I noticed that over the years, a familiar pattern kept happening. The same thing happened over and over again, only with different people. We would start out as best friends one-on-one, hanging and doing everything together. Then without fail, best friend always ended up being a closer friend with someone else that they preferred hanging out with more. This pattern followed me all the way into adulthood. It bothered me tremendously. I struggled with understanding what had gone wrong. This pattern was the beginning of my battle with abandonment issues.

Like I said before, I have always been a loner, but if I had a friend or boyfriend, I was completely unequivocally loyal to the friendship. But for some reason, I never found that same loyalty reciprocated. More and more, I began to feel unhappy with myself. I reasoned in my mind, that I must not be good enough, that there must be something wrong with me. Over and over I made tremendous effort to show people that I was good, and could be that one great friend, only to end up disappointed and hurt.

I remember a lot of lonely days of not being invited or included in events or outings with people who I thought were my "friends". I remember being friends with people and I would introduce those friends to other associates, next thing I know, they became better friends with each other and I was getting left out. Boys I really liked rejected me or chose me second over someone else. You can only imagine the confusion and pain I felt from that.

By the time I was in my 20's, I had built walls up around my heart. Not wanting to let anyone near it but then I always found myself breaking down and letting people in that ended up hurting me. There were a couple of guys I let my guard down for only to get stabbed again. It was an insane roller coaster ride that I rode on for many years.

Unknowingly, I was energetically attracting the same

1 DECIDE

type of friendships and relationships from people who would abandon and reject me. We are designed similar to magnets. We attract what we are or what we focus on. As long as this area of my life remained unhealed and un-dealt with, it would continue to repeat the same pattern. Over the years this same scenario would replay itself consistently, only with different people. I finally learned the problem was within me. I needed to recognize the pattern of negative behavior that was going on within and heal it.

Today, I still struggle with having defense walls put up for coping and protection, but I'm more aware of the toxic behavior I was unconsciously releasing. In knowing this, I am able to focus on this particular area of my life and do the work of undoing the negative energy that I was unconsciously putting out. I've learned to recognize and replace the negative thoughts with positive affirmations and actions towards myself so that I can attract positive energy in return.

Because I am more aware, my energy no longer attracts toxic friendships based on my neediness for validation. I am now attracting healthy and whole relationships. As I have healed, this awareness has applied to my business and family relationships also. Toxic energies are being removed that I no longer resonate with or am energetically incompatible with.

In my business as a hairstylist, I have had several clients that have dropped off over the years. Many of those clients were toxic. I have noticed that the clients I still work with, are in alignment with where I am in my life today. My financial situation has continued to remain stable even with the loss. Although, that portion of income is no longer coming in, ironically, other financial blessings have manifested in various ways that have not been negative or stressful and have allowed me to continue on as if those clients I lost never existed.

I had to humble myself and admit that I was the common denominator in carrying the toxic behavior that I experienced over and over. Now when I recognize something or someone is toxic, I will remove myself from the situation much quicker and reexamine myself for any remnants of lingering toxic traits.

I also see that by being conscious of this revelation, I've been able to change my patterns and thought behavior to a more positive way of thinking.

I honestly did not realize that I was the connecting factor in attracting toxic relationships. My perception of people who I felt treated me like I was not good enough, were all mirrored back to me based on the negative thoughts that I had about myself of not being good enough. I attracted people who cosigned with this subconscious belief to make sure that what I was telling myself came true.

Although this was my experience, happiness can be examined and defined in various ways. The dictionary definition of happy is "feeling or showing pleasure or contentment". It is hard to believe that no one feels or shows pleasure or contentment. What I have learned is that happiness is very broad and it means something different to every individual.

For example, I love petting a puppy. This activity brings me total happiness, but for a few of my friends, petting a dog means extreme fear and anxiety, because of the fear that they have for dogs. Another example, being content at home with a good book is happiness for one person, but to

1 DECIDE

another, it could mean boredom and displeasure. Therefore, instead of the question being "are you happy?" the question might need to be, "what makes you happy?"

Now that you have heard my story, what about you? Are you contributing to your unhappiness unconsciously by attracting toxic situations? Could it be based on the energy and toxicity you could be carrying within and emitting into the atmosphere that eventually manifests in negative outcomes?

Now is a good time to start reflecting on negative situations that you have experienced in the past leading up to the present that has become a pattern in your life. Are you a giver or taker? Do you seek validation and approval in order to feel happy? What makes you happy but the same negative outcomes keep happening?

You can break this down into several compartments such as, financials, relationships, careers, extracurricular activities, moral values etc. What are your most important core values when it comes to your happiness? Only you can decide what makes you happy and when you are clear about your happiness, you will be able to consciously make better choices and also relay that information to others.

I remember an incident one time where this rang so true for me.

Valentine's Day was approaching. I let the man that I was dating at the time know that I was not really into Valentine's Day. However, he wanted to give me a gift. I told him my favorite flowers are the regular fresh gerbera daisies that you can get from Walmart, Kroger, or Publix for about $8-$12.

But, in his mind, a more expensive the gift would

probably impress me more and show me that he was a good person and I would like him more. Therefore, instead of taking heed to what I said that makes me happy, he listened to the florist at the flower shop who talked him into getting the premium "Rose Package" which made HER very happy.

Now remember that society has told us, all women love roses, diamonds, designer handbags and shoes etc. They say that we would appreciate and be happier getting those items. With a lot women this may be true, but I am not like a lot of women. Anyway, he decided to disregard what I said that I liked and chose to get The Rose Package deal that came with one dozen red roses in a vase, a box of chocolates, a small teddy bear, a card, and a balloon all for well over $150.

Valentine's Day finally came and the items were delivered to my job. He was so proud of his purchase. Although I was appreciative of the gesture, I could not honestly say I loved the gift. Later that week, the roses died, the chocolates made me feel guilty for indulging, the bear had no home on the bed of this almost 40 year old grown woman, and the balloon was deflating.

I respectfully told my friend that I appreciated the effort but I also was truthful and explained why it was not a good idea to be swayed by someone else who did not even know me, but only wanted to make a sale. I communicated how important it is to listen closely and hear what people are saying verbally and non-verbally when it comes to their specific ideas to what enhances their happy place.

We should not seek approval from others by showering them with expensive gifts, being overly attentive, or using persuasive words we think people want to hear, knowing that when behind closed doors, it is only to soothe the

1 DECIDE

self-ego that needs to be needed.

Toxic relationships often form because people think the outcome will somehow play out differently if they just put a little more energy in their efforts to show others their "goodness and loyalty". Trust me, if the gesture is coming from a place of wholeness and not neediness, others will know that it is genuine because energy does not lie.

In reality, our ego is begging for validation because we do not think better of our own selves. Awareness and healing of toxic behavior will never happen until the inner man is dealt with. We should NEVER look for validation from other people to feed our pride and ego into being happy nor should we attempt to make someone else happy with gestures that will seemingly make us look good in the eyes of others.

Ultimately, happiness is a choice and a state of mind. Everyone will have a different perspective on the topic. It is important that you are not sabotaging your happiness, with negative thoughts, consciously or unconsciously. The key is knowing what makes you and those you encounter happy, so that you can articulate this to others when necessary! Otherwise, society will choose your happiness for you and oftentimes this route leaves most people unsatisfied and unfulfilled.

More Ideas for a happier life:

- *Gratitude.* Science has found that expressing gratitude leads to a happier life. Gratitude releases dopamine and serotonin levels in the brain which are neurotransmitters that give us feelings of contentment. Gratitude pro-

motes optimism, strengthens relationships, and your expressions of gratitude can become contagious to those around you.
- *Surround yourself with things that make you smile.* Watch videos of puppies or kittens. Be around like minded individuals. Eat good food with good company. Read or watch a film that will have you laughing. Take a drive at night with the sunroof back while listening to good music. Do whatever makes you smile and have a feeling of peace. Choose those things.
- *Forgive Yourself.* Forgive yourself for being critical, judgmental and harsh. Write down negative words you have spoken over yourself and then burn or throw the paper away. This symbolically represents that those words are no longer in existence or apply to you today. Do not hang on to anger or hurt. Be compassionate towards yourself even if you have to have a talk in the mirror and give yourself a hug.
- *Be conscious of negative thoughts or deeds.* Toss the negativity out as soon as it shows its face. Shift into a higher vibrational place using positive words and actions.
- *Don't focus on material or worldly gain.* Money and material possessions don't bring lasting happiness. They may bring temporary pleasure but not true happiness. Just look around at people who materially have it all, their lives are as much of a struggle as anyone else when it comes to having inner peace.
- *Find Friends that will hold you accountable.* Friends that aren't afraid to challenge you or hold you accountable. They will love you more than those that will let you stay low level or mediocre. Keep the type of friends that may

1 DECIDE

hurt your feelings with the truth but will not appease you with a lie.
- *Do activities that you enjoy.* Whatever that looks like, do it. However, be mindful of destructive or dangerous activities that could hurt you or someone else.
- *Look for the positive lesson in each encounter you have.* The rude cashier, the homeless man begging, the child throwing a tantrum in the store. Whatever it is, there is a lesson if you pay attention and look for it.
- *Hone in on your core values.* Your core values will keep your heart and mind centered and balanced. You will become protective of what you watch, listen to, and the company that you keep when your core values are solidly in place.
- *Visualize.* How and who do you want to be 3, 5, 10 years from now. What does your life look like? What are some steps that you can start today that will bring you closer to that goal? See yourself where you want to be and who you want to be. Direct your thoughts around those ideas.
- *Seek counsel or therapy.* If you find yourself struggling to find the happiness, joy, and peace you desire. Outside help may be needed to help you navigate through this new way of living.
- *Take small risks daily.* Taking small chancces or risks outside of your norm will help you to get used to shocking your comfort zone so, when it's time to take bigger risks, you are more apt to do so.
- *Stop worrying about what other people think.* There is no need to seek approval from others. You are the only one that should be validating your moves.
- *Stop comparing yourself to others.* Regardless of what

someone else's path looks like, keep the focus on your own journey and path.
- *Invest in YOU.* Become your own cheerleader. Invest in yourself with things that will push you to be a better you.
- *Stay committed to the process.* Take inspired action daily by learning something new, doing something different, or improving upon what you already have going on.
- *Pour your heart into working on you.* Self-improvement is hard work. Others can offer support but you and only you, can put in the true work.
- *Failure is not bad.* Do not, I repeat, do not beat yourself up, it happens. Get back up, dust yourself off, learn, grow, share and inspire others from your failures.
- *Don't dwell on the past.* Only look forward. The past is just that, the past.
- *No more victim mentality.* Quit feeling sorry for yourself and stroking your ego that comforts this mentality of "I have been done wrong".
- *Don't give up.* There is always a struggle when change is taking place, however, we are usually stronger than what we give ourselves credit for. Fight the good fight of faith. You are an overcomer. Toughen up when it is time to go to battle. Be strong and courageous. Have a Joshua spirit to take back your life. (Joshua 1:7)
- *Be patient.* Success in happiness will not happen overnight. It is a process.
- *Set Boundaries.* Speak up for yourself when people try to cross your boundaries. Stand firm and do not let people treat you less than what you deserve. Setting healthy boundaries keeps you accountable to yourself.
- *Help others.* When you run into someone who could use

1 DECIDE

a little help and you have the ability to do so without compromising your own happiness, help them. You will feel happy that you made a positive contribution in the world. Side note: be sure your motives stay pure and they are not tainted by self-righteousness.

As you put some or all of these tasks into play, be kind and gracious to yourself and do not judge yourself harshly if you mess up or totally fall off of the wagon. Remember the path to happiness, confidence and freedom, is a journey similar to a marathon. It is not a 100 yard dash race.

Be Confident and Free by recognizing your strengths and weaknesses

Have you ever taken out time to recognize and acknowledge your strengths and weaknesses? Most people can rattle off answers to this question when it's related to their work or career life during a job interview. But outside of a job interview, can you answer this question as it pertains to your daily life?

Most of us cannot. One day I decided to sit down and really think about this. After much thought, I was surprised at myself with what I came up with. Without overloading you with a whole list, I will just mention one strength and one weakness as an example.

One of my top strengths is that I can be open and honest about my vulnerabilities. But, one of my top weaknesses is overthinking after I have been open and vulnerable. Then I become insecure after I have been transparent. I will replay in my head how I should not have been so open and then begin to play out the worst scenarios that could possibly happen as a result of my honesty.

Oftentimes, we will highlight our strengths but hide our weaknesses. However, In order to become confident and free, I believe recognizing and acknowledging strengths and weaknesses go hand in hand. You cannot highlight one and ignore the other. Our strengths and weaknesses are what mold and shape us, they are a part of our value system. They will help decide the different paths we will take in life.

Have you ever known someone to take the easy route opposed to taking a path that will highlight a weakness, but potentially build character? I'm sure we are all guilty of this behavior of not wanting to appear weak.

However, after going through the Dark Night of the Soul, I was forced to face my weaknesses and build up strength in those very areas that I would normally like to dismiss and avoid. It is a very humbling process, but the overall outcome and growth has been worth every bit of pain and tears that I cried.

Do not run from your weaknesses, embrace them with the intention of experiencing growth and character development.

Be Confident and Free by Dismantling Past Beliefs

The enemy, also known as Satan, the adversary, the evil or wicked one, will always come after your mind first, to attack. Whatever we believe or not believe, our mind is always working and it is up to us to decide what we will believe.

When we are asleep or awake, we are always taking in information or downloads. Whether they are through thought, observation, or receiving, we will always be suscep-

1 DECIDE

tible for the enemy to come in and attack the mind. The adversary can show up in various ways that could powerfully influence the mind. The mind has the power to talk you into or out of doing anything, be it good, bad, or indifferent.

These mind attacks can take place and manifest through a passing thought, by daydreaming, during sleep, in conversation with others, watching TV, listening to music, overthinking, depression, and the list goes on. Because our minds are vulnerable to attack, it is very important to guard your mind as much as possible by being in tune and aware of what we are exposed to and what we are thinking. Mindless walks through life are a playground for unhealthy thinking. What do I mean by our minds coming under attack? It simply means whatever you dwell your thoughts on, good or bad, they can manifest.

For example, a murderer has typically thought about killing many times before he actually commits the act. He may start out fantasizing and watching shows that involve murder. Then he may act out by killing a small animal such as a bird or squirrel. Then it may evolve into killing bigger animals such as cats and dogs. Then the thirst becomes stronger and it may evolve into an actual murder of a human. The bottom line is it started as a thought that was not dismantled and struck down from the beginning.

A less extreme example could be a woman who daydreams daily about what her fairytale wedding will look like. She has probably thought about it since she was a little girl, reading Cinderella and Snow White in her storybooks. When she finally meets her "Prince Charming", most or all of her ideas were mainly focused on getting married before a certain age, having a beautiful diamond to showcase, the wedding ceremony, what the wedding decorations and venue would look like. And to top it off, how impressive it would be in the eyes of others.

In many cases, the thoughts are focused so much on the fantasy of the wedding itself, rather than acknowledging any red flags the person she's going to marry is displaying. This becomes secondary or bypassed altogether.

The wedding of her dreams comes true, but then mysteriously after the wedding ceremony, reality kicks in and the problems start. The expectations begin to emerge out of the cracks. Suddenly, Prince Charming does not seem so charming after all and five to ten years later they are at odds and have grown apart. As a result, the couple is coexisting miserably or divorcing.

How many times have you thought of something and it eventually happened? Again, because the enemy knows how our mind works, it is easy for him to slip in and plant thoughts for his evil purposes. If we guard our mind as much as possible, oftentimes we can recognize and "feel" when something is off or when it does not sit right in our inner spirit.

Long gone is the idea that the enemy is red, evil looking with horns and carrying a pitchfork. The enemy can show up looking as sweet and as innocent as an angel. He can plant thoughts that also seem innocent and harmless, but ultimately they are not for our highest good.

From birth and throughout life we all have been subjected to certain beliefs passed down to us from many sources. Our family, friends, strangers, teachers, bosses, tele-LIE-vision, and the government to name a few. We have all been exposed to some sort of influence that has majorly shaped

1 DECIDE

our belief system.

Our parents were commissioned to teach us right from wrong. Our religious affiliations were to teach us love, compassion, forgiveness, and faith. Society taught us persuasive views on various subjects such as politics, racism, education, history, and the like. But the only issue I have is, how do we decide whose thoughts are right... or wrong? Whose religion is the "true" religion? Which political stance is the right one?

The African American experience and history will be interpreted differently from the Caucasian history and their perspective. Native American history or any other cultural history will probably be interpreted differently by others. Even World History is not exempt. Each account will be a different experience for each group and that is not even addressing it from an "individual" perspective.

With all of this influence that has been passed down to us, can anyone honestly agree on what is the real truth? This is a ripe playground for the enemy to do his work. If he can get into the minds and hearts of us the people, his influence can be powerful.

This led to my very first thoughts of becoming Confident and Free. I began looking at how my belief system was controlling a good part of my life. I decided that I needed to dismantle certain beliefs that no longer served me or aligned within my spirit. If the belief no longer resonated with my purpose, I had to make tough decisions of letting go and follow my intuition and heart, regardless of what anyone else thought about it.

If you find yourself feeling similar to how I feel about certain passed down beliefs, I would encourage you to get silent, go deep within and ask yourself your honest thoughts or feelings about what you have been taught by your parents, school, society, friends etc.

Beliefs questioned:

When reflecting on our history in America. I was always taught that this is the GREATEST country in the world until... I traveled outside of the United States. I found that people abroad are no different from people in America. Almost everyone, no matter where they are from, possess very similar ideas. Most people believe family is important, living a decent life is important, striving to make livable wages, eating good food, and having an overall desire for happiness are all important. All of this mattered regardless of race, creed, religious beliefs, etc. The only differences that I mainly saw had to do with the differences in culture and each individual's upbringing that contributed to their core beliefs.

My question has always been: "if individuals were brought up to believe a certain way, but none of us existed when these beliefs were established, how then, can we prove who is right and who is wrong if all of our certain beliefs were passed down by generations before our existence?"

With this mentality of, "I'm right and you're wrong", comes the great divide, creating religious, political, and cultural wars because everyone thinks their belief is the one and only true belief system. People have literally lost friends and family from this because they could not agree to disagree about their belief system.

For example, in the American political system, it's the Democrats vs the Republicans that causes a major divide. Each thinks their group is the only true, right, and reason-

1 DECIDE

able political party. Now, political division has been created among the citizens. God forbid if you don't identify with either group, and you declare that you are a libertarian or nothing at all, then you are a moron in the sight of those two major political parties. I have heard people call other people stupid idiots simply because they believed something different. Even more disturbing to me is the fact that many of these people from both parties have declared that they are Christian and have strong moral values. In this particular scenario, who is right and who is wrong? That is the grand question that keeps us divided because of different beliefs.

I also began to reflect on all the racial inequality still going on today in America. As I write this book, in 2020-2021, we are experiencing a global pandemic with Coronavirus Covid-19. Protests and riots concerning police brutality, murder, and racial injustice within the current American judicial system against African American men in particular, have caused an uproar all over the world, allegedly.

This and many other happenings both personally and not, made me start questioning what I actually believed. In whose opinion, makes America the best country in the world? I am so glad to have a strong interest in international travel. Not only for my own personal experience, but to also get exposed to as much of this world as possible. I have spoken with many world travelers, as well as others, who are either from other countries or have lived abroad. I must tell you, from the stories I have heard and from my own experience gained from the little bit of travel I have done, my knowledge was not paralleling with the history books I learned from. Keep in mind again, this is based on MY experience and opinion. It is not necessarily a fact.

Can you begin to see how our personal belief systems could be skewed? If you talk to another person, their ideas and experience could be totally opposite of mine. Who is right and who is wrong?

Again, as I began to ask these critical questions and do my own research to find answers, much of what I grew up believing I have dismantled and done away with. I am no longer naively believing things just because that was what I was taught or exposed to by others. This includes information from my family, the government, church pastors, teachers, or whomever.

My approach now is to ask questions and search for facts, not opinions. Or, I will base some of my beliefs by situations I have had personal experience with. However, even with all of that, I am still being careful to keep an open mind in knowing that some things I will never know or be able to understand or have solid facts to back it up. I simply have to rely on faith, hope, and continue trusting the process.

With that being said, I challenge you to ask yourself the hard questions that you have wanted answers for. Begin to do your own research and more importantly, what is your gut deep down saying about your line of questions? I will be totally honest though, you will not receive an answer for every question. Many will remain a mystery until the end of time.

The advice I give myself is to live honestly and in my truth. I challenge myself daily to have integrity and to be as authentic as I can be. Even if it will affect other people, either in a positive way or not so positive way I will stick beside it as long as it is my truth. I can only be responsible for SELF and no one else.

2

Surrender

BE CONFIDENT AND FREE BY BEING MENTALLY HEALTHY

For a large part of my life, I have specifically prayed to have a stable and healthy mind. My family, on both sides, have members who have suffered from mental health issues. Some were professionally diagnosed and others undiagnosed, but you just know there is something not quite right. I had to recognize that I "could be" susceptible to mental health issues due to: biological (genetics, brain issues, substance abuse etc.), psychological (emotional, physical, sexual trauma etc.) and environmental (death, divorce, family dysfunction etc.) factors, but I also recognized that I have complete divine power and control over my mind.

I have learned that whatever I focus on, can grow and become my reality. We must understand that our mind can be our most powerful weapon or our most powerful enemy. If I spend my time dwelling on the idea that I have a good chance of having mental illness issues, more than likely I will get exactly what I focus my thoughts on. I had to surrender to the belief that my mind is and will always remain healthy. I had to surrender trying to control outcomes and begin trusting the process of the journey.

There were two areas of my life that I especially paid close attention to. I was sexually abused as a child (touched inappropriately by an adult family member) and emotional trauma (from death, divorce, abandonment and rejection). For a long time I was dealing with these emotional traumas that I never knew existed because I did not have a name or title to associate with my feelings. It was not until after my experiences with my sister's death, my church sister's death, and my uncle's death where I was triggered into the spiritual depression I described earlier in this book, known as the Dark Night of the Soul.

I knew I needed to find answers and find them as quickly as possible. I felt as if I was losing my mind and literally going crazy. Sometimes I even had suicidal thoughts, but fortunately, they were few and far in between. Mainly it was a complete dissatisfaction with life as I knew it. Everything in my life became meaningless with no more purpose. I was dissatisfied with my relationships, career, church, how I related to my family, everything. I am not saying I was having a nervous breakdown, but I was extremely overwhelmed and depressed. I became isolated and I cried a lot.

I was vulnerable and my mind could have been easily manipulated by my very own thoughts. Instead, I took control over my mind. Yes, I was sad and I didn't want to get out of bed most days, but my awareness remained alert. I knew I had to get myself together somehow. I made up my mind to take action. I sought out things that would help me. I researched and read articles. I found methods to calm my

2 SURRENDER

mind and offer me some relief. I kept being proactive instead of succumbing to my thoughts and feelings.

This was the point where I began to view things differently and question everything that did not make sense to me. I began digging deep within and a lot of truths were revealed, not only about myself, but everyone around me. I discovered that I was living a lie, which in theory, made me a liar. I saw very vividly the lies that I was surrounded by. This was a very hard pill to swallow. To realize a significant part of my life was a lie.

I began to relate to people on a whole different level where I practically begged for authenticity and realness. What I have discovered is that unless you have a life changing experience or you are naturally authentic, people would rather keep living with lies. Why? Because everybody lies and it is easier than facing the truth. The truth can hurt and people don't like pain. I understand it and I have compassion for those that aren't ready to do the work just yet.

Mentally, it makes it really hard for me to be around fakeness and lies when I can see right through people so clearly. It does not make them bad people, not at all. I try very hard not to judge people but to accept who they are because I was once in the dark also. But in my present effort of living a more authentic life, it is like trying to mix oil and water, it will eventually separate. Because of this separation, I no longer resonate with my old way of being. Many things and situations were associated with that former being.

Sometimes when you go through major changes, what you used to do, you can no longer do. Who you used to hang around you may have to wish them well and let them go. The Bible uses the analogy by saying you cannot pour new wine into old wine skin. There is a very high risk that the old wine skin would tear from being dry and brittle after fermentation when new wine is poured into them.

Sometimes you simply will not be able to hold on to old things as you evolve in life. Your mind will have you tormented and torn by the conflict. You become aware that there's a need to make changes, but your mind will give you every reason why it is not a good idea to let go of that toxic relationship, or to let go of that job that under-appreciates your talents and keeps you stressed out. Your mind will have you wanting to give up or commit suicide than to face the pain and pressures of life. You have to get your mind in line with what you know is best for you. If you do not, your mental health is at risk. You can only be tormented for so long, before you either snap or you change.

My interests in different activities became more authentic. I could no longer entertain hanging around certain people who carried a different mindset than mine. Even with physical activities, I have always been curious and adventurous as a child, but I remember being told "stop", "don't do that", "you can't", "you are going to get hurt", and other phrases. Because of my environment, I felt compelled to sort of suppress the adventurous side of myself. Once I became free, I began to live my life on my terms.

To some, I am viewed as quite radical. Many people have used the term fearless. My idea is just to live my life confident and free whether others agree with it or not. I was determined to live out the rest of my life in freedom and authenticity. I was no longer going to conform to societal norms that other people were more comfortable with. I decided that I was the only one that could live my life on my terms.

Naturally, I did receive some push back and criticism, but I did not care. My happiness was more important. MY mental health was even more important.

BE CONFIDENT AND FREE BY REVISITING PAST SUFFERINGS/TRAUMAS: FORGIVE AND HEAL

Along the way on this conscious and intentional journey to become Confident and Free, one of the biggest things you will have to face head on, is being vulnerable by revisiting your past. Your past is as recent as one second after reading this sentence, all the way back to your birth. For some people, they will go into their past or past lives (incarnations if that is something they believe in).

Personally, I went into my childhood as far back as I could remember.

One of the most significant conversations I had with my sister Audrey, was one of forgiveness. In my research, both spiritual and medical, I learned a lot about my sister's illness. Autoimmune diseases are basically the body attacking itself, sometimes triggered by stress.

From a spiritual standpoint, allegedly, autoimmune diseases are considered to be a form of rejection towards self because the body turns against itself and attacks itself. After experiencing rejection from other people over and over and over again, one will begin internalizing that pain. Mentally and emotionally, a person will begin to see themselves as worthless, unlovable, etc. The mind will begin to believe this lie whether consciously or subconsciously.

After a period of holding onto this belief, it can manifest itself into the physical form of sickness and disease. This type of illness is a mystery to medical doctors and they can only treat symptoms. There is no medical cure. Personally, I believe there is no medical cure because if we say, hypothetically, an individual is rejecting themselves because of emotional and mental stress, which ultimately breaks the body's immune system down, the root cause is a spiritual breakdown from lack of self-love.

There is no pharmaceutical medication available to make you love yourself. An individual would have to intentionally and actively practice self-love, believe and have faith that they will overcome the struggle. That is a spiritual cure, not a medical one. Notice I did not mention religious healing. The reason why is because I have seen countless people stand in healing lines at religious functions.

They would have the ministers to lay hands on them, pray for them, and have prophetic words spoken over them, but internally the struggle with self-hatred had not been addressed. I personally believe that they needed a mind healing first, before any physical healing could stand a chance of being successful.

It is not because I believe prayer does not work, it is because prayer has to have action in order to be activated. Once religious people exit the prayer line, many do not intentionally take action after the service is over, in order for the prayer to be answered.

For example, if you are praying for healing from high blood pressure and you get in the prayer line, once you get out of the prayer line, you must agree with God that you have received healing and then do your part for the healing to manifest. Your part includes actively changing your mindset for the healing to completely manifest. This begins by

2 SURRENDER

changing your ancestral agreement that high blood pressure runs in the family bloodline. Reject this claim spiritually. Change your approach to your nutritional diet. Add an exercise program. Get plenty of rest. These are all intentional actions to accompany the prayer, but the mind must discipline itself to stay focused and on course with the planned actions. Most people stop at the prayer line and then get angry at the preacher or God because they were not one of the ones who received a miracle. Now all of a sudden the preacher is a scam artist or God does not care about them. No, there comes a time when personal responsibility must be taken. Remove the fried and fast foods from your diet. Find peaceful and calm activities to de-stress. Pray with an expectation that your body is healing itself as you are being proactive in taking the necessary steps for healing.

Could it be possible that we can create our own realities by creating suffering from our mindset and experiences from our past? When left unaddressed, eventually it could turn into a disease? Medically, we already know that stress can trigger the body to physically cause illness, even mental illness.

After presenting this possibility to Audrey, I asked her to take a walk down memory lane and list as many people that she could think of that she could possibly be holding unforgiveness, resentment, and bitterness towards and forgive them for what they did. She wrote down people who had rejected her, abandoned her, lied, cheated and stole from her. She even found forgiveness for those that told the truth, when she may not have wanted to hear or accept the truth at that time.

Not to get into any names, I'll just say her forgiveness list was very long. We went as far back as her childhood up to that present moment. We wrote out every name and the offense. She first forgave herself, then she forgave each and every person who had wronged her, from family, friends, ex-coworkers and ex-husbands, and even the doctors she had started resenting because they were constantly giving her bad news about her condition. It was sad and heartbreaking to know that she carried so much internal pain.

After this exercise with Audrey, I myself had been compelled to do the same exercise by confronting my past offenders that I had internally held grudges or resentment against for years. As I went back into my childhood memories up to the present, I found out, my list was long also. In all transparency, the hardest person to forgive was myself.

When confronting unforgiveness, there may be those that you will need to call or go see in person and have an honest conversation with them. With others, forgiveness may be done through making a decision to change your heart towards them and by letting the offence go.

I was shocked at myself. I began to remember people who I had long forgotten about on a conscious level, but my subconscious remembered them quite well. I retrieved this info by going into a deep, quiet meditation, focusing only on this particular subject.

Some other memories that were triggered hit me deeply. I was sexually abused by a relative at a very young age with inappropriate touching. It happened only once that I can recall but it still made an impact on my life negatively. Another time, I was around preteen age and an older male exposed himself to me and a friend. I buried both incidents and never told anyone. Periodically the thoughts would resurface in my mind as I got older, but I would repress it back down, never dealing with the trauma.

Going into meditation and prayer with my past was a VERY powerful and emotional experience. It was an ongoing event to say the least. There were several dark days and a lot of tears during this process. Healing did not happen overnight either. I became depressed off and on for at least two almost three years straight. Again, as stated earlier in the book, it was an extremely painful process but it was truly necessary, as I look at myself today.

God used some very special vessels to come across my path (unbeknownst to them) to continue triggering deep rooted emotional issues that needed massive healing. Whether it was a word or an action that stirred up what was brewing on the inside of me, it was enough to let me know I needed to address it head on. Although irritating or painful, I am very thankful that I was forced to face past issues that I never or rarely ever talked about.

I discovered where I had been rejected, abandoned, and used in relationships, by past boyfriends, dates, even friends and family that I had placed on high priority, more so than they had ever done for me. I saw where I had very unhealthy and toxic attachments to a few individuals that I sought validation from.

I also saw how I had become emotionally "detached" towards relationships, friendships, or situations and events going on within society that I should care about. I no longer FULLY gave myself or my attention to any relationship or friendship that was truly meaningful for fear of experiencing the pain of abandonment and rejection.

Funny thing is, the very few times that I did let my

guard down for people, these were the "special vessels" God used to stab me in the heart and hurt me every single time until I learned the lessons I needed to learn. What's even crazier, is that I saw very clearly how I needed to experience the pain that I felt. These experiences, no matter how painful, would get me to a place of being sick and tired of being sick and tired of going through the same pain over and over. I finally surrendered and faced the pain head on so that I could fully heal.

Low self-esteem, low self-worth, abandonment and rejection held me hostage and kept me bound for many years. I realized how I had continued to experience the same scenarios over and over but with different characters in each scene.

I continued with sabotaging behaviors conjured up in my mind from overthinking. I created narratives in my mind that made perfect sense to me, although never based on facts. Focused beliefs and perceptions occupied my thought process. For example, if I noticed a friend that I talked to regularly, and then one day, I didn't hear from them, my mind started working overtime. I wondered if I said or did something that offended them. Did they find a better friend? Are they distant because they no longer liked me?

I discovered that the longer you dwell on these types of thoughts, like magic, subconsciously the self-prophecy would come true.

What I did not understand at the time was that we are energetic and spiritual beings having a human experience. Our energy can attract or repel. Have you ever noticed when a woman or man seems to attract the same type of person over and over again? A woman whose mother was abused by her father seems to always attract physically, mentally, emotionally or verbally abusive men.

Men who were raised by a single woman that babied them and had no strong male figures to guide them into manhood, always seem to attract women or single mothers who are willing to settle and take on more responsibilities than him, in order to have even just a piece of a man around. Usually these women had absent fathers or fathers that were physically present, but maybe not emotionally present. Humans tend to try and compensate through others what they may have lacked in their past, only to attract the same type of people over and over.

I found myself attracting broken people in my life who had been abandoned, rejected, or abused as well. Not necessarily physically but emotionally. Like me, they had nothing to pour from an empty cup. We were just broken souls attracted to and attaching to each other because of familiarity. When it seemed like the relationships were getting too close or too uncomfortable, one would run, the other would cling, chase, or hold on for dear life out of fear of experiencing loss. We were abandoning or rejecting the other, but in reality, also abandoning and rejecting our own selves in the midst. Each party was a mirrored reflection of the other.

When a person or situation mirrors another being, it digs up and presents trauma that triggers the individual. Once this happens, the person has a choice to either confront and face the pain, or run away from it, burying it deeper. Only to keep repeating the cycle until one is ready to face it and heal it once and for all.

Learning about trauma and how it can affect your

entire life choices is very interesting once you begin to recognize and research your own dysfunctional and codependent patterns.

This is why it is so important to go within and face your sufferings from childhood and adult traumas. If they are not addressed and dealt with, you will be like a hamster on a wheel. Running full speed but never getting anywhere. You will continue to repeat the same patterns and cycles until your awareness kicks in. Then you will begin to recognize the patterns and be faced with the choice of confronting or ignoring them.

What traumas do you have that you may be repressing? Do you have emotional baggage perhaps from abandonment, rejection, jealousy, or envy? Perhaps you have experienced some physical trauma such as sexual abuse or even spiritual trauma from cults, brainwashing, doubts about spirituality, or even your very existence based on upbringing or lack thereof. How have these issues affected your personal life? Dating life? Marital life? Friendships? Relationships overall with people in general?

My abandonment and rejection issues ran deep. I wanted to be accepted and validated. I always desired and wanted to be chosen first, but seemed to always get picked second or not at all. This also played out in almost every area of my life from potential romantic relationships, friendships or job promotions. No matter how much effort I put into people or situations, the results seemed to always end the same. Being chosen second, or being faced with abandonment, rejection or both. Romantic relationships never panned out positive long-term. Close friendships often turned into mere acquaintances after a few months or a few

2 SURRENDER

years.

What I began to understand about energy, was that I was repelling and self-prophesying unconsciously that I was not good enough. That I was not worthy of real and true friendships. That I would never be chosen first. Although I desperately desired meaningful friendships, my energy repelled it from happening. I was self-sabotaging any relationship that could have promise. All of this was happening energetically on an unconscious level and it was all laced in fear. Although I wanted to have successful friendships and relationships, fear sabotaged most of them. Again, the relationships that I did manage to have for longer periods of time, were often toxic, one-sided or codependent.

With men, it never seemed quite equal or at least close to being equal. It was always one or the other going out of their way with very little reciprocation. Oftentimes the men were suffering from different insecurities themselves. They would be emotionally unavailable because of some type of trauma or abuse. The friendships with women were often one-sided. I usually put more effort into them than they put into me.

Up to this date as I write this book, I have only had five or six really good friends in my lifetime that put in as much effort into me as I into them. The reciprocation has been very close to equal. With everyone else it has been way out of balance and totally lopsided.

As a result of these experiences, my desire waned towards forming friendships especially with females. I had resolved in my mind that I did not want them nor need them, but, still secretly desiring to have meaningful friendships. It would especially bother me when I would see other females with life-long friends who got together to hang out, travel, share birthdays, or other special events regularly and consistently. Again, the few of the friends I did manage to have during those times, most of them were toxic and unhealthy.

I remember my former friend *Naomi. Naomi would always dump her problems on me. When she called she barely asked how I was doing before she would jump in fully with her life and her problems. I would patiently listen, and periodically give her advice if I could get a word or two in. I continued to repeat this cycle over and over for years. I used to feel completely drained after each encounter with her, but I was that friend who remained loyal. This went on for over 20 years until one day, I said, "I can't do this anymore". I began to let her know, if she was not going to do anything about her situation she had been dealing with all those years, she could no longer talk with me about it.

Of course she got mad at me, accused me of being mean and that I had changed. She literally told me that I wasn't a nice person anymore because I put my foot down and set boundaries with her. I could not believe how somebody could dump on me for years and then get mad when I got fed up with feeling like a trash can.

I could not blame her completely though. Why? Because I had trained her early on, that it was okay to use me as her metaphorical trash dumpster. I allowed her to do it. I let her get used to that role and now after 20 years, I suddenly wanted to switch it up and change things. I had no choice but to understand her position. I had to take full responsibility that I had trained and created that monster. However, I did not have to continue to participate in a toxic friendship. I had to stand firm for my own mental health's sake.

2 SURRENDER

After that, over the years she kept in touch from time to time. Every year or two I would get a call and she would test me in small doses. I could read right through the fake "I just wanted to check on you my friend". No, she still was not interested in my life. It was always about her and her life. The very last time she called, I had enough of the entire friendship. I did not make myself available and continue to give her the benefit of the doubt. I simply watched the phone ring and let it go to voicemail. I stood strong in my boundaries. She left a message. When I listened to it, I made a decision right then and there that I was no longer interested in having this toxic friendship. Yes, we had known each other for many, many, years, but as far as I was concerned, that time was up.

My new journey towards self-love meant ending relationships that no longer serve me at my highest good. I have to continue to uphold those boundaries no matter who it is. Even family members are not allowed to cross them.

Facing traumas whether with people, death, or other tragic events can take a toll on one's psyche. If not dealt with. It will follow you through your entire lifetime. I made a choice to confront and face mine. I did not want to be like Audrey. I didn't want to carry such heavy burdens and potentially develop an illness and then die because I was afraid or unaware of emotional baggage that was never dealt with.

I didn't want to waste a lot of precious moments living life in fear of being abandoned, rejected, lacking self-love, and being always in doubt. It was not worth it to me any longer. I wanted to live Confident and Free! This chapter is so critical when it comes to living life Confident and Free. Make it a priority if you are ready to conquer your fears and stop suffering from traumas. Of course it seems easier to bury and NOT deal with them. However, this will leave us with a part of our life's happiness in limbo or in stuck mode because we refuse to be honest with ourselves. It is so much easier to be the victim. I know firsthand! I thoroughly enjoyed being in victim mode. It gave me an excuse to remain in my comfort zone of being one of the most emotional, non-emotional persons that I know, allowing me to blame anything or anyone for my failures.

I still have triggers that rise up and I have to continue to go within and heal those areas that are still unhealed. There have been people who have acted as catalysts in my life. Again, usually unknowingly, they will do or say something that will seriously trigger and provoke an unhealed area. When this happens, it is usually a very painful experience.

Triggers will continue to happen, until those dark fears are faced. Now that I am aware of when and how triggers happen, it does not take me as long to acknowledge and address the issue. I will reiterate, healing does not happen overnight, but spending enough time being in the present moment allows one to observe feelings and pinpoint when, how and why the trigger happened.

My encouragement to you is to not be afraid any longer. Quit running from yourself. Why? Because wherever you run, yourself is still going to follow you.

Oftentimes, people or events will show up in your life to trigger that hidden pain. That is God's way of showing us we need healing. If you begin actively looking or researching your particular issue of pain, resources will start showing up that will help you through the healing process.

2 SURRENDER

Some of you may choose professional therapy, or various other ways to heal and that is okay. The point is, get whatever help you need to bring your heart, mind, and soul into complete peace and balance.

I personally did various self-care activities such as: Healing Touch therapy, salt cave sessions, hanging out in nature, equine therapy, and meditation. Other activities that bring me happiness and peace are, visits to animal shelters and rescue parks that rehabilitate animals (I love animals). I read self-help books, study bits of psychology and metaphysics. I pray, journal, and do physical exercise. Whatever I can do to increase self-love and peace, has become my focus.

Seek wisdom on what you need to do for yourself when triggers happen and when you need to find peace and healing. Make the decision today that you will no longer suppress unwanted feelings of hurt and pain. Make the decision that you will face those hurts and pains once and for all.

There will probably be destructive voices inside your head that will try and dissuade you from taking action. They will bring up all the reasons why you should just let bygones be bygones. There will be all sorts of reasons to justify why continuing to repress the pain is the better course of action.

Again, you have to make an intentional decision to move forward in your healing. This is a very personal decision to make. It has to be right and feel right for you and you alone. Nothing or no one can force you to confront anything that you don't want to confront.

If you are ready for healing, I challenge you once more to examine your life, your life choices, and your past behaviors very closely. What patterns do you see? How has your past contributed to those patterns? Paying close attention to the patterns will enable you to get to the root of the problem and come up with answers and find solutions. By doing this, the first step towards healing is to acknowledge the sufferings. Stand on the outside of yourself or emotions and observe your thoughts and feelings towards the pain. Then allow yourself the freedom to tell yourself that it's okay to finally make accommodations to let… it… go…!

3

Visualize

What does it mean to visualize or have vision? The dictionary definition of vision is the ability to think about or plan the future with imagination or wisdom. When I was seventeen years old, although I was still in high school, I could see myself being a hairstylist. However, in my family, attending college was kind of expected. I am the youngest of three and both my sister and brother were college graduates. My parents only made it through high school, so it was automatically expected that I would follow in my older sibling's footsteps.

Visualizing my life was basically centered on what I had been exposed to. I come from a small rural town in Georgia and in the 1970's and 80's there was not a lot of exposure compared to an urban city setting.

Regarding race, we were not diverse. You had blacks and whites only. The whites were the majority. In my graduating class of 99 students, there were less than ten blacks and one Filipino. This will kind of give you an idea of the race ratio. Today, it is much more diverse.

There was not a lot of positive influence or encouragement concerning our future. My parents could only teach what they knew. My Dad was military and travelled the world, and my mom was a country girl that had never left Georgia. We were mainly encouraged to go to school and get a good corporate job that would provide security, if the military was not an option.

There was still something inside of me that let me know I was meant to do more than just have a job that would pay the bills. Now granted, I tried college and the corporate job setting with a major bank. I quickly learned that I was not a good fit for either. But quietly, I always enjoyed styling hair. I also had an aunt that was pretty successful as a "beautician". I explained to my parents that I was unsure of what I wanted to get a degree in. I asked if I could leave college and go to beauty school until I figured things out. They obliged. I did not know how things would work out but I had a vision.

My first step would be to go to beauty school, next I would then find a mentor. Ironically, both of those ideas happened. As I moved forward in my vision, I met people in the industry that opened doors for me as I continued to grow. Each year I had a different objective for growth and again it would happen. I visualized making enough money to own a home, and then to invest in real estate, that happened too. Each idea built itself upon the previous ideas.

Having a vision is always the first step in planning your future goals. Now don't get me wrong, there will probably be some hiccups and bumps in the road along the way. There will more than likely be some twists and turns that will seemingly take you off course. I have never seen anyone's vi-

3 VISUALIZE

sion remain on a straight course the entire time. But overall, the core center of the vision stays in tack.

You have to be able to see with eyes of faith where you want to be and what it will take to get there. It is basically trusting in an unseen victory. Ask yourself where do you see yourself in the next year, or two? Start with small doses of short-term goals that will lead up to the bigger goal.

As you continue to visualize you also have to see yourself having breakthroughs with each challenge that comes about. Visualize yourself getting breakthroughs in healing past traumas and pain. Whatever comes next with your life's destiny and purpose, the cycle of breakthroughs should never end when you have a vision in place.

If you are married, your household should have a vision for each new phase as you grow. It should never become stagnant or complacent. You both should be challenging each other to level up individually and as a partnership or team. If there are children involved they should be included in the vision as well.

As you begin to practice the exercise of visualization, you are simultaneously cultivating your inner self. You are becoming more centered with what you want and desire in life. You will become picky with whom you allow into your personal space. You will analyze your current relationships and decide who is meant to stay because they add value to your life and who to let go because they either add no value or they suck life and energy out of you.

A good friend once reflected on the story of Jonah in the Bible. Jonah had a calling (a purpose to fulfill) by God on his life to warn a certain people about God's wrath but Jonah rebelled because he did not want to go where God told him to go. In fact he got on a boat and went in the opposite direction of where he was supposed to go. Then there came a mighty storm on the ocean and everyone on the entire boat was at risk of dying.

The others knew this storm was a result of Jonah being disobedient. They had to make a decision to throw Jonah overboard in order for the storm to cease. So that is what they did. They got rid of him by tossing him over into the raging sea. Immediately the storm calmed and Jonah was taken up into the belly of a whale and was spit out three days later after he finally had come to his senses to do what he was destined to do.

The point of this story is that you will have to decide what Jonah's you need to toss out of your boat if they are a hindrance and not a help in your life. Or perhaps you are Jonah, and you are not walking in the purpose or calling that has been placed upon your life. Don't rebel and be forced to do it. Freely give of yourself to serve those you have been called to serve no matter in what capacity. Big or small.

In cultivating your vision, you may need to do something for growth such as going back to school or taking a couple classes, or doing self-study on your own. You may need to start by writing your vision down and making it plain (Habakkuk 2:2). Cultivating your vision is having an idea to focus on as you take action steps to make it happen.

4

Ignite

BE CONFIDENT AND FREE BY GETTING COMFORTABLE WITH YOURSELF

During my struggle with depression and isolation, interestingly, these moments also ignited me into having an extreme interest in getting to know myself.

Getting comfortable with yourself simply means learning to love the real you and totally enjoying your own company without the need to have others fill a void of you being alone. In my observation over the years, I have learned that there are a whole bunch of individuals that do not want to be in the company of their own self. If one does not identify specifically as an introvert or ambivert (mix of introvert & extrovert), most likely, sitting with self is extremely difficult for those identified as extroverts.

Most of my peers that struggle with being alone are extroverts. Extroverts typically get their fuel and crank by being around others. They usually prefer larger groups or crowds. They love having a good time with people. As a matter of fact they are energized by being around others.

Introverts on the other hand usually like certain people, enjoy solitude, and if other people are involved, it is usually a very small group or setting. Introverts get their charge of recovery by being alone.

However, even if you are an extrovert, still consider spending some alone time with yourself often. Focus on the positives that can come with being in your own company. Even if you start out small, like shutting off your phone to get 30 minutes of alone time to reflect, meditate, pray, read, write or relax.

The more you spend time with yourself two things will probably happen. 1) You will find that you actually enjoy it 2) With intentional focus, you can learn a lot about yourself. I have met people who literally do not enjoy being alone. My first thought is why not? What could be the underlying reason behind that? When digging into one's background a bit, particularly going back to childhood, sometimes the issue stems from being neglected or being left alone a lot, which would trigger that memory of abandonment and it could lead to different forms of anxiety and fear.

Others could simply be uncomfortable being alone with no specific reasons. Some may get bored when there's no one to talk to or they could begin to feel anxious by doing nothing or by not having anyone around. For those people, I would suggest having a plan. Designate certain amounts of time for an activity that could be done alone, such as, napping, sitting out in nature or whatever else you might like to do that is calming, relaxing and removes you away from all the noise.

Although I enjoy good company, I have always been the loner type. When I became intentional on spending quality time with myself, I found that I preferred and enjoyed being alone the majority of the time. It gave me the opportunity to meditate, reflect over my past, and create changes for my future. If I am spending time with others, it helps me even more if we are on the same frequency and mindset.

Again, I challenge you to start getting comfortable with yourself. I believe that you will find it not only beneficial for your body and soul, but your mind will benefit and begin to align itself accordingly.

BE CONFIDENT AND FREE AND STIR UP YOUR GIFTS

What do I mean by stirring up your gifts? So far, we have touched on, deciding to be happy within, recognizing strengths and weaknesses, dismantling past beliefs, and getting comfortable with yourself. After doing all of this, you should begin noticing that you are becoming more aware and open-minded about the possibilities that lie ahead.

You should be compelled to take a look at your life and begin to really question, "What is your true purpose for being here on this earth?" What are the things you want to do but have not because you have a lack of belief in yourself? We all have a purpose and a destiny, but many people struggle trying to figure it out. Oftentimes, this is because we operate in the mindset of what society expects of us, instead of what we truly desire, deep within.

I once read a Facebook post that asked the question: "What would you be if you had followed your childhood dreams?" The answers from the commenters were varied and quite interesting. It seemed that very few people followed through with their actual childhood dreams. I have discovered not only from my life, but from many others, that our childhood dreams will often reveal our life's purpose early on, only to be dismissed by societal brainwashing.

So what is societal brainwashing, you may be asking? Let's look at an example from my life.

When I was around 15, I had a keen interest in Psychological ideas. I wanted to be a Psychologist. My second dream was styling hair. My dad grew up in an era where you either went to college or into the military. He had a niece who majored in psychology and had a hard time finding work with just a Psychology degree. In his limited knowledge of various ways to make money with a psychology degree, he advised me to not choose that area unless I was willing to endure 11 years of schooling to earn a PhD. That squashed my dream. My 18 year old mind could not phantom going to school that long.

I decided to quit college and follow my second dream of becoming a celebrity hairstylist and business owner. Well, I did become a hairstylist running my own business, and I got the chance to style a couple of local celebrities and discovered that I had no interest in having a celebrity clientele nor the headache that could come along with that.

Ironically, although I did not pursue a degree in psychology, being a stylist gave me the experience of the title. I often listened, sometimes advised, and more importantly challenged my clients to look within for their answers by presenting various perspectives on their situations. Over the years I have been told multiple times that I am appreciated more for being their personal therapist. The hairstyles were secondary.

I truly believe that as our personalities are shaped and usually solidified at an early age. Our true core self somewhat knows what fits as a career or purpose fulfillment. How many kids have lived and breathed singing after being exposed to the Sunday school choir, school chorus, or even the ones bold enough to sing on the city streets, but never pursued being a professional singer as adults?

What about that child who was always tinkering and taking apart their toys and putting them back together again, but as an adult never pursued a career in engineering, building and repair, or becoming an auto mechanic etc.

More than likely those dreams were suppressed because someone or something said that they should pursue something else. A suitable career that is guaranteed financial stability or something that is more practical, like a teacher, doctor, or manager at a big corporate company is what I would hear people talk about. I cannot begin to tell you how many people I know that hate their jobs, but stay because it provides a good paycheck.

Even for me, my dad told me that getting a good job in psychology was almost impossible with just a four year degree. He based this off of my cousins' bad experience in that job market. No one knew to explain to me that there are various and creative ways to make money doing what you love. Unfortunately, I had not been around any creative entrepreneurs.

I never pursued Psychology from the standpoint of obtaining a degree. I thank God I still had an opportunity to practice parts of psychology indirectly in my hair business from: my own personal study and research, being very intuitive and discerning, possessing good common sense, and having the natural ability to be a critical and objective thinker which allows me to see situations from multiple angles. I have been blessed to have wisdom to decipher the root causes of the client's issue.

What gifts do you have that you have not nurtured or applied to your life? A good way to begin thinking about this is to get a journal and start writing down things that you are good at and that you enjoy. Specifically mark the ones that are strictly hobbies and those that could be possible careers. Then ask yourself if there was no possibility of failure, would you pursue it? If you analyzed worst case scenarios, would it still be worth pursuing even if it was a side business instead of a full-time commitment?

Whatever your gifts are, regardless if they are a career or remain a hobby, they are meant for you to share with the world in some capacity.

I remember seeing a Facebook post one of my cousins made. She was a former color guard girl and coach. She posted a video of her doing a color guard dance to a gospel song. Just from the comments alone, many people, including me, were blessed and encouraged to see her willingness to stand in her yard, dance, record herself, and post it to social media was very inspiring and bold to some, especially those who are afraid of writing a post much less pressing the submit button with a video of themselves. Was it something that every viewer enjoyed? Probably not. The point is, your gifts will not be for everyone but for the ones they are for, those people will be very grateful and will enjoy that you shared it with them.

Your gifts could be shared on social media, in a small or large church, in a school, at a local community event, family reunion etc. It doesn't matter. What matters is that your gifts are not meant to be hidden and only for you to enjoy. You will never know how you could bless or change someone else's life by putting yourself out there. Don't hoard your gifts, share them with the world!

LIVE CONFIDENT AND FREE

5

Conquer

BE CONFIDENT AND FREE BY LOVING YOURSELF

YOU HAVE PROBABLY HEARD THE PHRASE "YOU cannot be successful at loving anyone until you learn to love yourself". This rang so true in my life. I never realized how much I did not love myself until after my spiritual enlightenment journey began. I often wondered why I was unsuccessful with relationships whether friendships or family. The answer was simple. I did not have a loving relationship with myself. The opposite of love is hate. Did I actually hate myself? When I look back on past behaviors and responses, I could admit that there was definite evidence that I hated myself.

I know some of you may be thinking that hate is such a strong word, and you're right, it is. However, in my search for truth and authenticity, I had to face some hard facts. Hating parts of myself was admittedly true and I had to conquer that part of my attitude toward self and begin to express grace, mercy, and forgiveness for treating myself poorly.

Whenever I would use sabotaging behaviors to destroy a relationship, it confirmed to me that I did not think I was worthy or lovable. Subconsciously, I was preaching that I was not good nor lovable enough for myself. In doing so, I attracted and manifested exactly what I wholeheartedly believed deep within. It does not matter if you say "I love myself" verbally out loud one thousand times. If the core belief is opposite of that, the energy will attract exactly what we believe inside. Until you can train the subconscious mind to line up with the conscious mind it will overrule the conscious mind.

Some people tell themselves destructive negative nonsense consistently. This can lead to low self-esteem and low self-worth. They will accept doing unacceptable behavior, such as not setting healthy boundaries out of fear of losing someone. They may allow themselves to be a doormat for people to walk all over them. They may allow their bodies to be a dumpster for another person's sexual pleasure.

Until we align ourselves with awareness, we may very well remain in the dark of our negative belief system and continue to blame others for our lives being sad.

A great way to start becoming aware is focusing on the negative outcomes we think people or life circumstances are throwing at us. The Mirror Recognition Exercise is a great place to start. For example, look directly at yourself in the mirror for at least one minute, then follow that with asking yourself and answering questions such as the following:

If I feel abandoned by someone, ask, how am I abandoning myself?
If I feel rejected, ask, how am I rejecting myself?

5 CONQUER

If I feel insecure, am I insecure? The mirror will reflect how I am insecure with myself (most people cannot look at themselves in the mirror for a prolonged amount of time without starting to feel uncomfortable.)
If I feel someone is avoiding me, ask, how am I avoiding myself?
If money is scarce, ask, how is my relationship towards money? Am I thinking with a scarcity and broke mindset?
If I seem to never reach a certain level of success, how am I subconsciously sabotaging success coming forth? Am I operating in fear, or speaking negatively over the outcome?

One instance I can remember was when I was coaching beauty professionals in business and was not getting the traction that I wanted. Although the stylists and barbers loved what I had to offer, I noticed that I kept attracting people who didn't want to pay my fees. I would say, "They know they need what I offer, but people always buy what they want and beg for what they need".

    Now although this statement has some truth to it, I believe subconsciously, I was self-sabotaging my success from attracting great clients because I was still holding on to the belief that these beauty professionals did not think my material was worth buying. When in fact, deep in my core, I was the one who believed and thought it was not good enough.

    Why? Because I struggled with the past belief that I was never good enough to be chosen first. The same way I was not chosen first in grade school and high school for childhood games or friendship. Deep down, I felt that more popular beauty pros would be chosen before anyone would choose to invest in my services and products. This self-doubt repelled success from coming towards me.

After enlightenment, instead of detaching from my feelings, repressing or pushing them down (which I was very good at doing). I learned to embrace those feelings. I allowed myself to feel the pain and emotions by stepping outside of myself "observing" those triggered feelings and how I initially would have reacted towards them. Observing allowed me to detach from reacting to the emotion but not allowing me to ignore the problem. This awareness gave me the wisdom to know that I needed to show myself unconditional love, not judgement and criticism.

As I began to practice awareness and address each issue as it arose, I noticed that I started attracting better people. Better events, situations, and even unexpected money started coming my way.

How have you sabotaged positive things from manifesting in your life because of a past core belief that you may not have been aware of? Write them down. Learn to observe and tackle the situation head on. A few suggestions towards loving yourself are:

Be kind and gentle with yourself, not critical or judgmental
Reprogram your mind with daily positive affirmations. Allow them to soak into your spirit.
Practice a few minutes a day, acceptance of yourself. See (visualize) yourself as good, loveable, smart, and accepted by others also.

The more you continue to speak positive words over yourself, the sooner you will begin to believe it. The more you

5 CONQUER

begin to believe, others will follow that same energy and will believe in you as well.

BE CONFIDENT AND FREE: BEING AUTHENTICALLY YOU

Did you know that authenticity is highly valued? Overall, many of us, if honest, do not like or trust people that come across as fake. In most cases we may avoid such people. Being phony reduces the credibility of a person. Although most people hate a phony, it's quite interesting that we live in a society where being fake has become more accepted than those who choose to keep it real.

In my journey towards living Confident and Free, being authentic is imperative. If I cannot be real with myself first, I could never expect others to keep it 100% real with me either.

Along my spiritual awakening journey, two people in particular challenged me to keep it real in any given situation. At first it was a bit scary. Why? Because so much of our daily life consists of lies. Not the "huge" lies, but the small justifiable "white lies" we tell.

I found through research, that the average person is lied to 10-200 times a day. And the average number of lies told every day by one person is 1.65. Another study said that it was found that 60% of people lied at least once during a 10 minute conversation and told an average of two to three lies. People tell a considerable amount of lies in everyday conversation, says psychologist Robert S. Feldman.

Why do people lie so much, we may ask? According to Feldman, people lie to impress other people. He said, "women typically lie to make the other person they are talking to feel better. Men typically lie to make themselves look better". As I began to examine my own life, I became well aware that I did not always tell the truth when presented with the opportunity to do so. I began to also notice other people lying about things for no good reason at all. Just lying to be lying, from my perspective.

As I really began to pay VERY close attention to myself and others, I quickly became annoyed. I could not believe some of the things I lied about just to save face. For example, by trade I am a hairstylist. I have done thousands of heads during my career. In the midst of those thousands, there have been plenty of clients that I absolutely hated working with. Instead of being honest by letting them know that our client/stylist relationship was not working for me, I continued to act as if I really liked and appreciated them. But what I really wanted to tell a few of them was to go to Hell and to kick rocks all the way there!

Instead, I put on a fake mask and acted as if all was well, when in reality I was boiling on the inside. I wanted to fire many clients on the spot and tell them to get out of my chair, but I was the type of personality that did not like confrontation. I was never quick and slick with the tongue. Because I was slightly on the bashful and quiet side, I never spoke my mind until someone absolutely backed me in a corner and I had no choice but to defend myself.

I found myself saying YES to things I wanted to say NO to! Why couldn't I just be honest and keep it moving? Because that would be too much like right!

After I was challenged by those two individuals to "just be real", It raised my awareness and I began to observe situations where exercising my truth needed to be made

5   CONQUER

known.

I began to exercise my power of truth with my job, with other people, and with decisions I needed to make. These decisions needed to resonate with me with where I was, at that moment in my life.

Years ago, I remember meeting a guy and coming into a potentially new relationship. The attraction was mutual intellectually, mentally and physically. I really liked him because we had a lot of things in common.

I later began to see that there were things about this potential relationship that did not align with my core values. Because I liked him and the things we had in common, I found myself considering to ignore the red flags and go against what I knew I wanted and what I didn't want.

Would I listen to my logical mind and see things for what they really were and move on, or listen to my emotions instead? My gut intuition said, love yourself first and remember your self-worth. He was a smart guy, and if he didn't desire to see the value that I brought to the table, it would be a lost cause anyway.

I chose to listen to logic over emotions.

After setting aside my emotions, I licked my wounds from my injured ego and chose to let go of the idea that we would be a good match. Not only did I need to protect my mental health, but my physical health as well. Being stressed out is never good for the body.

In the long-term, choosing myself was more important than desiring to be validated by someone who was not valuing me anyway. I had suffered enough from past abandonment and rejection, to be back peddling because of this one man. That spoke enough volume for me to let it go.

My ego and pride were severely bruised, and my mind judged me harshly. I even guilt tripped myself for being naïve believing that I could change someone just because I we had a lot in common. Thankfully, I found the strength to love ME more.

Not living my truth and standing up for myself could have set me back so far emotionally and mentally, that I might not have ever recovered. I would have compromised my moral values and ignored my intuition.

I had to stand in my truth and not pay attention to the noise in my mind and ear. They both can be very deceptive. I couldn't worry about "what if?" I couldn't worry about someone else capturing his attention. I couldn't worry about feeling that I had lost. However, I remembered, you can't lose something you never had.

I had to get out of my emotions and logically reason with myself and trust the process that if it is meant to be, it would come back to me with no struggle and no compromising my worth.

I could not put myself through unnecessary suffering. I went on with my life, detaching from any expectations or outcomes. Loving myself made everything okay!

Too many times us ladies ignore what we know to be the truth deep down. We tend to hang on to relationships longer than we should, hoping if we just pray harder, sacrifice more, and be there for them that it will work out. Funny thing is, men are simple, and they know early on if they want to build something with someone. If they are in a place of readiness, they go after what they want. There will not be any questions or hesitations.

I can also relate this to my business in the beauty

industry. In 2020 during the pandemic, our businesses had to shut down. I had a part-time position working for a company doing lash extensions and they decided to open the doors again after only 6 weeks into the shut-down. It was before the country or many other businesses had reopened. The state of Georgia seemed to be on a quest to outdo other states and be the first to open back up.

I had to make a decision. My gut was saying hold off, do not be quick to rush back to work, but my mind was saying go back to work and make some money. As I began to sit still and get quiet so that I could really listen to my gut feeling, it kept saying no. I was not willing to risk my health or safety for a $10 an hour with great tips part-time job.

Long story short I didn't go back...EVER. Not because it wasn't probably safe, eventually, but because I am learning more and more to listen to that still, quiet voice called intuition. If I was honest, I did not like the job nor did I truly want to go back anyway. Prior to the pandemic I was already wrestling with the idea of letting it go. Shutting down was the pathway for me to leave and focus on my true passions.

Most of the time your gut intuition will guide you correctly. It was not about the Governor and media reporting that our businesses could reopen. I simply felt it was not right for me to return to that job.

What are you faced with that the REAL you hasn't stood up for? Begin to look over your life and the decisions you have made, did they bring you peace or suffering. What are you faced with right now that you are struggling with in making the best decision? I would suggest you get away from everything and everybody, get quiet and still. What does your inner most self say? Do not justify the situation with reasons like money, loneliness, being accepted or liked. If there is a hint of the slightest uneasiness, that issue should not be taken lightly. It may require deeper thought to come up with a solution that will bring your body and mind to a place of peace.

Inner peace is the ultimate goal. When you start standing up and begin being the REAL you, you will experience a peace you have probably never felt before. You will feel empowered and accomplished.

The more you practice being the real you, the easier it will get. Before long, you will feel strong enough to stand up for what you truly believe to be right for you. If there is anything that does not resonate with you, you will be able to easily assess it and make a decision or determination based on what YOU want and it will not be by anyone else's ideas or requests.

Be Confident and Free: Understand the Power of Joining the "NO" Ministry

You have put your dreams and ideas on hold because you became a wife/husband or mother/father. Your children became the focus. You began busying yourself with every single activity your child talks about even though they have not shown a genuine interest in the proposed activity. You do not want to say no to your child because you don't want to be seen as a bad parent. You find yourself giving in.

Your spouse, family or friends are dismissive of any dream or idea that you desire to explore. They are flat out unsupportive and have shot down every idea you have presented, but want you to give your undivided attention to

5 CONQUER

their dreams and ideas.

Is it hard for you to say no? Do you feel as if you will be perceived or judged as being mean, harsh, or indifferent? Does saying no make you feel like the bad guy or girl?

Let's learn from Warren Buffet who said, "The difference between successful people and very successful people is that very successful people say no to almost everything."

For many, that small but intimidating word can cause big and major problems when it's not freely utilized. I have encountered more people than not, in my personal and working life, that truly struggle with saying no. I personally had a hard time with saying no for a very, very long time. I would find myself saying yes to things that I had no interest in doing whatsoever.

In my business as a hairstylist, trends come and go. Two particular trends I honestly hated doing were hair weaves and braiding styles. The entire process was excruciating. They were way too time consuming. I pricked my fingers constantly with the sewing needle. My hands and wrists would get tired. The only thing I enjoyed 3-4 hours later was the cash I received as pay. As much as I hated doing those services, I always seemed to let someone talk me into doing those type hair styles.

One day, I had a "come to Jesus talk" with myself. I would ask myself, why in the world would I continue to do these styles if I hated doing them? The only logical answer that I could come up with was because, I did not want to say no. Worse, I justified it by focusing on the money. I did not want to be the stylist that turned down a client and their money.

I had to resolve within myself that all money was not

good money, especially if I had to compromise my core authentic self. Good business practice in my opinion, is to stick with what resonates with the core self. If I did not do this, I would be depriving myself of being at peace. Resentment could begin to kick in and it would start to affect the interaction between myself and the client. Why? Because from experience, when the client calls, I would dread picking up the call. Many times in the past, I would return a call back hours later, as I tried to pump myself up to be happy about making the appointment.

Eventually, I made the decision to completely stop doing weaves. I replaced saying yes, with a polite but firm no. I also had a backup stylist I could refer them to. This made my life and my business a lot more peaceful and meaningful. I only wanted to provide services that resonated with my core self.

As stated earlier, I struggled with saying no in my personal life also. There was a time in my life that I would change my plans or desires to accommodate someone else's plans and desires. I especially recognized this pattern in relationships.

I have always been laid back, easy going, and flexible. I did not even think or consider that my wants and desires were just as important as someone else's. There were many days I went out on dates and the plan was decided early on to see a particular movie before we arrived at the theater. It never failed, once we arrived, the plan always changed when the other person saw a "better" movie choice.

Instead of standing firm on the plan, I always relented and gave in to the new plan. Now there is absolutely nothing wrong with making last minute plan changes, but if you are

5 CONQUER

the one that is always compromising, then no, this is not okay.

Eventually, I started standing firm in my truth of saying no to things that did not or no longer resonated with my higher self. My low vibrational self was a coward. My higher self was confident in standing in her own values and truth.

Once we begin to stand in this power confidently, people will treat us better, and with more RESPECT. No doubt you will have those that will say you are being mean, but it's really just being honest with self and with those that we encounter.

For me, several people, including family, had to learn to adjust to this new and improved person. But, there were others that did not adjust to the new me. That was something I dealt with. If others could not see or respect my views, then oh well, I'm sorry, but not sorry.

Learning to say no is very liberating. It frees you from being in bondage to people and things that make you feel obligated to participate in. One time I made a post on social media about joining "The Church of No". I said that it was the best organized ministry I had ever been a member of and invited the readers to join me in my newfound ministerial walk.

Now this was meant to be comical in a sense, but I was very real within the context of why I posted it. I received several comments but the ones that were the most heart touching were the commenters that truly recognized they needed to be free from the bondage of being a "yes" person.

You see, many of us recognize that there is an issue. The problem is the guilt and fear that consumes us. We know that we need to change the toxic behaviors, but fear and being stuck in comfort zones will hold us back. Once we accomplish getting past the suffering we place upon ourselves, (yes each individual is responsible for the unnecessary sufferings they endure) and see that we are not legally or morally obligated to be people pleasers, only then, will the chains be broken.

Let me say it again, you are NOT legally or morally obligated to be a people pleaser. I don't care if it is your mom, dad, sister, brother, relative, friend, supervisor, pastor, or the President. If you are pleasing people based out of fear or guilt, it is not right.

Here is a list of six ways that will be helpful in standing in the power of saying no:

1. Examine the Pros and Cons of saying no in any given situation. Ask yourself pertinent questions. When getting to the answer, leave your emotions outside. Do not be concerned about your feelings. The decision made will be strictly from logic and facts on how saying yes or no will affect you later. Once you have weighed your reasons for saying no, stick to your guns and do not waiver. The more you practice this procedure, the easier saying no will become.
2. Set Healthy Boundaries. You cannot nor should you try to always be a people pleaser. Being a yes man is an outdated limiting belief system. Back in my parents and grandparents days, saying no was considered being rude in most cases. My grandparents, to my knowledge, rarely said no to company or people that they knew were respected citizens around town. My grandmother would cook Sunday dinner and no unexpected guest was ever

turned away even if they were "no good" scoundrels.
3. Put Yourself First. The best thing you can do for having any healthy relationship, is to take time and make yourself a priority. Women in particular, naturally are nurturers, caregivers, mothers etc. They tend to look after everyone else first and neglect their own needs. This oftentimes leads to unhappiness, bitterness, resentment, anger or frustration. Making a firm commitment to put yourself first, will cultivate stronger relationships. When other people know that they cannot just walk over you, expect any and everything from you, they have no choice but to respect that you have chosen self-love and self-care first. By doing this, you will actually have more love, energy, and sacrifice to give. Why? Because you will be able to pour from a full cup instead of an empty one.
4. Don't say yes just because you struggle with saying no. Saying yes is not the solution when you struggle with saying no. You will need to practice some simple techniques of how to say no with kindness and honesty, while being firm, leaving no wiggle room for someone to persuade you to change your mind. Try a phrase like, "I'm sorry but unfortunately I can't…" Avoid phrases like, "I doubt if I'll be able to…, or I don't think…" These phrases leave open doors for persuasion to occur and guilt will have you saying yes.
5. Practice. Start out practicing by saying no to low risk requests. Such as, a sales rep standing in Wal-Mart trying to sell you Direct TV satellite services. Say no to the lady at the kiosk in the mall that stops you and wants you to try out their amazing new hair straightening tool. Low risk situations will get you used to saying no and

strengthen you when encountered with the higher risk situations.
6. Do not say yes quickly. Get used to letting someone know that you need time to think about their request. The allotted time will give you the opportunity to analyze if it is a request you would like to participate in. If the person asking, gets pushy or does not respect your request for time, you have the right to get pushy with them with your request for time. People will test the waters of your boundaries and if you let them win, they will continue to treat you like a doormat because you are teaching them that you are exactly that, a doormat to be walked on.

Joining the No ministry will be one of the best decisions that you will make in life. You will feel more confident and free. No longer will people treat you like a pushover. No longer will you live your life full of fear and guilt. No more saying yes to un-ideal situations that do not benefit you in the present or long-term.

Be prepared to fail a couple of times simply because it will feel awkward to say no, when you are not used to it. Eventually standing your ground will become second nature. When presented with a situation you will know right away if it is something you feel comfortable doing. Guilt will cease. Second guessing will cease. The overall torment will cease. You will rest comfortably at night knowing that you are making decisions based on what is good and right for you. You will no longer focus on how you will be seen or judged by the other party. In fact, you won't even care what they will think about you, as long as you know that you are being true and authentic towards yourself first.

5 CONQUER

BE CONFIDENT AND FREE: HANDLING CRITICISM GRACEFULLY

Along this new journey you'll be walking in, be aware that not everyone will be onboard and supportive of the new you that will emerge. In fact I can almost guarantee you that someone will not be in agreement. Do not be shocked or surprised if the people closest to you are not the ones cheering you on the loudest. This is because in general, people typically do not like change. When things start switching up outside of what humans are used to or what they are comfortable with, resistance normally follows.

Your family and friends are used to the old you. Introducing the new you will be a major change for them. They will not understand why you are saying no when yes, is all they have ever known you to say.

When our awareness arises, we must take responsibility for our part in training people with how they have treated us in the past. The saying goes: "You teach people how to treat you". People who have established strong boundaries may get talked about but they are never disrespected in how they are treated.

The people who have mastered this skill have no problem with being criticized and they sleep well at night. If what is being asked does not serve them, they are at peace with not complying.

In handling criticism gracefully, we must not feel guilty for the decisions made for our personal peace of mind. It is not your problem that other people have a problem with what is best for you. There is no need to argue or defend your decision. Be confident enough to say no without giving an explanation, a reason or false excuses. Simply say a gentle but firm no, then let silence follow. This is a very powerful technique that will have people respecting your boundaries and they will back off.

Be Confident and Free: Stop Worrying About What Others Will Think

How many times have you denied yourself opportunities, based on what you thought other people would say? Does the thought of others thinking bad of you, give you anxiety? Perhaps, you know deep down inside, a major decision needs to be made, but you are conflicted and torn. What if that decision would impact others such as family, coworkers, friends etc. in a not so positive way, but the decision is best for YOU. What do you do? How would it make you feel?

I have been there. In fact I lived a great deal of my life being concerned about what others thought of me. I let it hinder things that I wanted to do, say, even believe. Fear of what someone else's thoughts were about me, gripped me more times than I care to admit. I come from a small town, and raised in a pretty well-respected Christian family.

How would my decisions affect my loved ones? What if someone becomes offended, or doesn't agree, or would think less of me by my actions?

I would torture myself constantly being concerned about judgement. It took me a long time to confront this issue, but after experiencing my spiritual awakening, one thing that stood out for me was that I realized I was in bondage in my own mind of how people would view me. I allowed worry to consume me about something I truly had no control over.

5 CONQUER

That's right we have no control over how other people perceive us or our actions. Things we cannot control, should not have control over us either. What we do have control over is our own mind and thoughts. That is really all that should matter.

I had a client once, named *Nancy. Nancy was a single, financially stable woman. She had accomplished many goals in her career. Nancy desired to be married and have children but her biological clock was ticking with no boyfriend, or even a potential significant other in sight. She had given in to all of the advice from other people. She was told to be patient, wait on God to send her a husband.

She was told he would show up in due time. She just needed to take her mind off of it and solely focus on her career. She had friends introducing her to the "perfect guy" who would end up being a jerk or incompatible. She tried this practice over a span of several years.

Nancy was now at a crossroad. At 38 years old, should she continue to listen to her friends and family by waiting for the perfect man to appear or would she entertain her unspoken idea of exploring a sperm donor? She felt in her heart she needed to make a decision but her decision needed to be based on her own desires, not anyone else's. Naturally, she battled with the thought of how people would perceive her or how her children would be treated, not having a "real" father. After many days and nights of research and long deliberation, she decided to go ahead with having a sperm donor. Nancy never shared her decision with any other person except one trusted confidant, her therapist. She waited to make her announcement until after she was entering into her second trimester. Of course some of her close friends and family were horrified, disappointed, and even angry with her decision. However, her decision and peace of mind was all that mattered. It was what she wanted to do.

She went on to deliver a healthy baby girl and a boy followed three years later. Overall, she was happy with her decision to have two beautiful children.

One thing I have learned in life, it doesn't matter if you do good or bad, great or terrible, there will ALWAYS be someone out there that will judge you negatively. All we can do is live life to the best of our own ability and not worry about other people who honestly, should only be worrying about their own lives.

One of my own experiences with this was when I was in Savannah attending college. I dated a guy who turned out to be quite abusive, verbally and emotionally. I broke up with him and tried to move on with my life. He made that very difficult, almost impossible. I realized I had a real life stalker who was not taking no very well. He was applying serious pressure and control over me. Each encounter became more and more aggressive, to the point I began to feel unsafe.

I never informed my parents of this situation. At the time, my 19 year old thoughts were, they would probably be mad, and disappointed. I assumed they would probably ask, "How did I get involved with such a guy?" Or worse, they might have gotten the police involved. I really did not know how they would respond.

I only knew that I had to make a decision about my future. Had I sought answers from my friends, I probably would have gotten a ton of different "you should do this.. or if I were you" advisors. The advice would have been endless.

5   CONQUER

Ultimately, I knew I had to ask Erica, what did she want and need to do? So after long thoughts about it, I decided to leave college life in Savannah and transfer to a school in Atlanta. After I did that, the harassing phone calls stopped and there were no more intimidating surprise pop ups with him showing up at my dormitory.

Another example of making a hard decision where I was worried about what others would think was when I was 24, and was faced with a marriage proposal. Despite having apprehensions about getting married, I was given an ultimatum. Either get married or we go our separate ways. I was under pressure and began to lecture myself on why it would be okay to get married. Every answer I came up with was to justify why I should proceed with getting married. Although I knew deep within, I was not ready.

Here are a few of my excuses: He was the only person at that time in my life that showed an interest in me. We had been dating eighteen months, therefore time had been invested. He had a decent job. He went to church. We enjoyed going to the movies and eating out.

The red flags I saw within the relationship, I chose to ignore. I feared getting married. While dating we argued and held grudges constantly and consistently. We were in couples counseling the entire dating period. We couldn't communicate nor agree on other major things that were required and expected in marriage.

Despite the red flags, I proceeded and walked down the aisle. As you can imagine, the same week after saying "I do", I knew I had made a serious mistake. Getting an annulment was always an option, but my pride and my ego would not allow that to happen.

LIVE CONFIDENT AND FREE

What would my friends or parents say? Also, I had spent a few thousand dollars on planning the wedding. I came up with numerous reasons why I should stay in the marriage. Unfortunately those reasons were not enough to sustain us. All of the red flags magnified 10x's greater.

Fast forward five years later, we ended up divorcing. I knew I was making a mistake but I allowed myself to be concerned with what others might say instead of going with my personal truth and acting on it. In all honesty, as I think about it today, I was using the excuse of what others might say, when truthfully, I was afraid of looking like a failure.

Sometimes we have to get out of our OWN emotions of how we think of ourselves. Emotional decisions are just as bad as deciding on things based on what we may feel others would think.

I am happy to say that these days, my ex and I were actually able to remain better friends than marital partners. He is still cool with my parents and we get along much better being apart as friends, than had we stayed together.

The decision to walk down the aisle was a mistake. Getting an annulment would have been the right thing to do. Deep down in my gut I knew both of these to be true. I chose not to listen to either and ultimately had to suffer the consequences of those choices. However, with every necessary event that we label a "mistake" is here to teach us lessons and to help us grow and mature; hopefully, for better decision making in the future, as we navigate this mystery thing we call, LIFE.

Whatever your situation is, be it a career move, a relationship, a change in spiritual beliefs, deciding to be free from living in the closet of homosexuality, or whatever it is,

5 CONQUER

you must make the final decision of what you think is best for your life. Be able to live with the consequences of that choice whether good, bad, or indifferent. Only you can determine that.

BE CONFIDENT AND FREE: HAVE A SUPPORTIVE ENVIRONMENT

Being around a supportive environment is very important, especially for your mental and emotional health. Having a friend or family member that understands you, believes in you, and encourages you is like a breath of fresh air.

This circle should be your cheerleaders but more important they should be your source for brutal honesty. They are not critical but will offer constructive criticism when necessary. They will be able to give you sound, logical advice, and wisdom, even if it means hurting your feelings. They desire only to see you succeed and win. If you fall or fail, they will be there to pick you up. They will encourage you to not give up, and will offer positive reminders and other nuggets that will add strength to your battle with the world and with your own mind.

Nine times out of ten, the world will be against you. Simply because we are in a herd mentality society where many will follow the crowd. They never question questionable things. They do as they are told by the masses.

To be confident and free requires a boldness that goes against social norms. If you are okay with the basic social standards then, being confident and free will only "sound" good to you. There will never be any real bold actions taken. Going with your gut, even when no one else is doing it that way, takes strength and courage. Having a herd mentality is not being confident and free.

For example, I have always desired to be an entrepreneur and own my own business. However, my environment consisted of parents, family and community where few went to college. Most had secure jobs that paid the bills and offered a basic but decent lifestyle. Staying at these jobs for 30 or more years until they were eligible to retire was normal.

Although some did not exactly "love" their jobs, they were secure with the every two week pay system that clothed and provided shelter for their families. Now don't get me wrong, there isn't anything wrong with this set up, however, it was not okay for me.

I always dreamed of styling hair as a little girl, but it was not exactly encouraged as a career choice. My parents lived in an era when, if folk who were privileged enough to go to college, found this to be their ticket to living the "American Dream". The thought that their children could possibly have a better life working for big corporations was ideal. I tried the college path, but it just did not fully sit right with me.

When I went away to college, I was majoring in business management and was working for a major banking institution in Savannah, GA. When I transferred schools from Savannah to Atlanta, I transferred my job as well. I was proudly making more money than I had ever seen as a young adult. I made approximately $450 every two weeks. I was doing great. I had my own apartment (in the hood) but hey, it was mine. One check covered rent, the second check covered utilities with a small amount left over for food, clothes when needed, and leisure activities.

It was not until I decided after four months of this

5 CONQUER

routine that I discovered GA State University and Nations Bank did not bring me peace, joy or happiness. I went back to my old idea from high school of being a hairstylist. I decided to quit college and attend beauty school. This is what made me happy. I managed to get a few clients from church to come to my apartment who were willing to pay me to do their hair. It was a great side income

As time went on, I ran into people who helped propel my idea of being a licensed stylist. I eventually graduated beauty school and landed a part-time job at a salon. I still worked my bank job because I was afraid of letting go of my security blanket. However, the salon owner saw potential in me. She kept encouraging me to let the bank job go and come into the salon full-time. After going back and forth about this opportunity, fighting with my mind, I decided to step out on faith and go for it. It felt like the right thing to do.

As God as my witness, my very first week in the salon full-time, I made over $600 with NO established clientele. I was only servicing walk-ins. To make a long story short, my hair career took off like wildfire! I continued to grow and managed to maintain repeat clients. I never looked back from that point on. It was my purpose and my destiny at that time in my life.

I share this story because it is the perfect example of being in a supportive environment that saw the potential in me and was willing to support, guide, and cheer me on as I navigated through uncharted waters. I would not have been brave enough to leave my secure, $425 every two weeks corporate job, if I did not have the push from someone else who believed in me.

LIVE CONFIDENT AND FREE

I went on to have a successful career in the beauty industry as a stylist, a cosmetology instructor, a public speaker and educator at major hair shows. I also became a published author, as well as a beauty business coach for over 28 years to this date.

I now have taken the same skills and approach to launch my life coaching business. My passion for helping women and (a few smart men), is to push and encourage them to live the life they have always wanted to live. This includes becoming the best version of who they are within and no longer being brainwashed to live according to society's standards of what is best for their individual lives.

Whatever you have to do and whomever you meet along the way, pay close attention to those that genuinely celebrate you without looking for anything in return. This is the circle you must surround yourself with. Sometimes this circle will only consist of 1 or 2 people but oftentimes, that is all you need to believe in you.

BE CONFIDENT AND FREE: FIGHT WITH FAITH

Fighting with faith means that in order to conquer and overcome all of the obstacles that will come your way as you move closer and closer to being confident and free, you will have to maintain a level of strength to not fall back into old patterns. This may not always be easy. Fighting against old ways, beliefs and habits will be a continuous battle of the mind until it becomes second nature to walk in the new shoes you have decided to wear.

In the past, you may have been told that you would never amount to anything or that you are not smart enough or good enough. These limiting beliefs may have hindered

5 CONQUER

or even paralyzed you. Fighting these negative remarks will require a faith that is not seen and a belief that no matter what, you will overcome them.

When you are faced with a situation that has you straddling the fence, slow down, take a deep breath and begin to ask yourself the important questions. Is the belief that you are holding onto, actual truth? Are there facts to back it up? Does this request or action serve you at your highest good? Will you have regrets surrounding the situation? Will the request or action benefit you in a positive way? Will the person or situation survive if you say no?

I believe one must take a moment, step outside of any emotions, review and analyze the request or action. When you make decisions outside of emotions, thinking logically and realistically, will make things a lot easier.

To help stay focused on conquering the challenges that undoubtedly will come your way, I found five practices that have helped me along my journey to remain in faith. They will challenge you to become the best version of yourself. You will not only live your best life, but it will also bring your natural gifts to the forefront. The world is waiting on you and your gifts to show up. Your gifts will have an impact specifically on those that need what you have to offer.

Before I go any further, I must make the disclaimer that offering your gifts to the world does not necessarily have to be on a grand scale. Sometimes we can get intimidated by the idea that our gifts must only be seen at state, national, or international levels. This is far from true. Your world could be your family, friends, children attending Sunday school at your church, or the homeless at a local shelter. Your world could basically be anywhere your gifts are needed. It could be as simple as speaking an encouraging word to the stranger in the grocery store check-out line.

Do not get sidetracked thinking your journey has to be grand in order for you to walk in confidence and freedom. What matters is that having strong faith in yourself and God makes all things possible!

Now let's look at the five different ways that you can expand on for growth and creativity as you stay focused and on track:

1) Identifying your mental and emotional blocks. Begin asking yourself questions where you feel some sort of hesitation. Is there a reoccurring fear that comes up? For example, do you question yourself on whether or not you are qualified or good enough? Go within and listen for the answer. Were you bullied in elementary school by students who said you weren't smart? Perhaps you had a family member to tell you that you weren't qualified, because you lack a college degree. Write down your questions and thoughts in a notebook and begin to sit with those questions and thoughts until you have identified the reasons for the hesitation.

2) Self-Love. Can you honestly say you love yourself? One way to identify this is to simply ask yourself: "Do I always put other people ahead of my own needs?" If your answer is yes, you are struggling with self-love. These "other people" often include spouse, children, family, friends, co-workers, church, etc. Almost everyone feels a sense of guilt in this category. Do you find yourself putting "you" on the back burner to fulfill something for someone else? Deep down within, do you feel obligated to honor requests, but

5 CONQUER

would actually prefer not to do them?

In my career as a stylist, I saw this lack of self-love a lot with my clients. They would try to take one day, to at least get their hair done. It never failed. The spouse would call last minute saying he could not pick up the kids from school because he needed to finish something at work. The client would cancel with me last minute and run to go get the kids. This would happen multiple times. So much so, I felt that the spouse oftentimes took the wife for granted.

It was perceived as no big deal for her to cancel her plans at the drop of a hat, even though it was not an emergency for him to remain at work either.

Before you all that have children jump down my throat, I am not saying that you should not sacrifice for your children. I am fully aware that that comes with parenting. But, what I am saying is that sometimes you must get selfish in order to see after yourself. If you are worn down, tired, and feeling less than attractive, that energy will spill over into your job, your family, and other relationships. Your entire life can be impacted in a negative way, in the form of bitterness, anger, and resentment.

I often tell people, if you are steadily pouring out of your cup giving to others, who is pouring into your cup filling it back up? Eventually you will become depleted. When this happens, the seeds of anger, bitterness, and resentment can begin to take root towards the very people you are always pouring into, but never getting anything in return from them. It is okay to set healthy boundaries for your self-care! Yes, even with your spouse and children. You should never feel guilty or make apologies for loving yourself.

3) Acceptance of self. You must have the faith to believe that you are uniquely and divinely created in the image of God. You have to know that you matter. Your voice should be heard, your unique personality should be displayed, your physical make up should be embraced, and your gifts should be shared.

We all have flaws because none of us are perfect. You must get comfortable with who you are! Accept and love your knocked knees, your broad nose, your skin complexion, your protruding forehead, your long neck, your stuttered speech, your thick glasses, your gray hair, your gapped teeth, your balding head, your fat belly rolls, your skinny legs, etc. Whatever flaws you do not like about yourself, begin to say affirmations that are opposite of the criticism you constantly point out and frown at.

Get in front of the mirror if you have to, and have some long meaningful talks with yourself. If you find that you have been extremely ungracious to yourself, be gentle, kind, and forgiving towards yourself. Forget about judging and continuing the criticism of bad talk about yourself.

Science and psychology has confirmed that positive affirmations are healthy and very effective. What I have discovered with myself, is that the more I embrace and accept myself, energetically, I attract other people who also see me in a positive light.

If you find yourself being overly critical of yourself, it is high time that you change that behavior. Have faith to believe that you will see a positive difference not only with how you treat yourself, but believe that other people will begin to see and respond to the positive change.

Our energy is real. If others are disrespecting you, fig-

5 CONQUER

ure out how you are disrespecting yourself. Remember, other people are simply mirroring back energy that we are emitting from the inside, whether it is conscious or unconscious.

4) Explore and add adventure into your daily life. I must admit I am an "adventure" junkie. I will try almost anything adventurous at least once. The judgement I received from others in my early years hindered my thirst for adventure. When I look back over my past, I had suppressed my natural love for adventure and allowed other people's fears and apprehensions to stop me.

Faith is walking into the unknown and the unfamiliar, believing that it will all work out somehow.

When I started intentionally adding some sort of adventure back into my life regularly, I noticed I was happier, more fulfilled, and less tense. I truly felt more confident and free. I personally need those doses of endorphins to be released. My personality requires it.

My adventures vary from extreme adrenaline driven activities to more calm activities such as sitting by the lake, reading a good book, writing, or simply engaging in conversation that challenges my intellect.

You decide what suits you and begin to intentionally incorporate different things or activities into your daily life on a regular basis. Step out on faith to live your life even if others do not agree.

5) Travel. This is one of my personal favorites because I absolutely love to travel. It has always been a huge dream of mine to travel the world and experience as many countries and cultures as possible. For me, traveling allows my

mind to expand beyond my environment and comfort zone. Wherever I go, I always set the intention that I am going to do something different and try my best to learn something different from what I have been exposed to or experienced. There is so much more out there than what my limited environment growing up allowed me to see.

I began traveling more. Mostly to states that were near Georgia. Robin, one of my former clients turned friend, is a traveling chick. Traveling with her increased my faith that I could go anywhere my heart desired. She gets the credit for expanding my love of travel. By her example, I have been to places I only dreamed or thought about visiting.

I have even travelled solo. Now that is a whole different subject especially dealing with the amount of projected fears from others that were piled on me! Again, it took faith for me to step out confidently and freely to not only travel farther distances than I had done but to also solo travel. Some of my best experiences were when I traveled solo.

Because I was open minded enough to switch up the usual routine, I was able to experience places that were very unfamiliar and I could see them from my perspective. By making the decision to do something different and willingly going against the advice from others, I feel like there are no more limitations as to what I can do, achieve or receive. Doing what I feel is best for me, takes FAITH!

6
Overcome
BE CONFIDENT AND FREE BY REALIZING YOU ARE WONDERFULLY AND FEARFULLY MADE

Walking in confidence and freedom is recognizing that you are created in the beautiful image of the creator God. We were created in a complex way. We did not just magically become who we are. We were designed lovingly. We are all different and unique.

We are meant to live a life of happiness, joy and peace. Somewhere along the way after our creation, we were introduced to things in life that no longer brought peace, joy, and happiness. We have been introduced to fear, hurt, pain, hate, disappointment, etc. After this introduction, we began to live life inauthentic and not in truth. Overcoming these negative experiences will be one of the hardest things you might ever need to do, but it will be worth it in the end.

When we become aware, we can make a decision to get back to that original state of peace, joy, and happiness. We will begin to see our self-worth again. We will begin to see the importance of practicing self-love, soon getting back into alignment with how we were originally created.

We all have been designed with unique qualities and talents that were meant to be shared and now is the time to stir up those gifts if they have been lying dormant.

You must embed into your brain that you have complete control of how you want to live out your life. Of course you will have some twists, turns, hills and valleys, but overall you can recreate your reality and live the life that you were created to have.

7

Embrace The New You

BE CONFIDENT AND FREE BY LIVING LIFE WITHOUT REGRETS

When I started my spiritual awakening and journey, I had no idea what I was about to encounter. The first stage was opening my eyes. Similar to how in the movie the Matrix, Morpheus introduced Neo to the Matrix. Basically, he took him on a spiritual ride showing him things that he thought were real only to discover everything around him was an illusion. Oftentimes an illusion is created all within the mind. Our thoughts, ideas, and perceptions can be manipulated and influenced everyday by different encounters.

Morpheus presented Neo with two choices in the form of a blue pill and a red pill. If Neo chose to take the red pill, that meant he would take a ride deep down into the rabbit hole and see things he has never imagined before. Truths would be revealed. If Neo chose to take the blue pill, this would enable him to go back to sleep and wake up forgetting everything that Morpheus had shown him and told him. He would go back to living life as usual.

In other words, he had the choice to see and experience truth which would allow him to overcome struggle and recreate his own reality or he could continue to live comfortably in a dream world with illusions that were persuaded by society, government, politics, and religion.

This world that we live in is a dream and fictitious but it all depends on your perception of your reality. Those that are not aware are easily led around like lost sheep. Living in a world full of illusions is often easier and more comfortable because it is what we have always known and what we are used to. To choose to live in a more truthful and authentic way, life is much harder. Mostly because this chosen lifestyle is going to go against the grain and challenge our entire existence and everything we have learned and been taught.

It is a lonely world, but given time and some understanding, it can be a wonderful experience walking in true freedom. There will be pain associated with this walk, but what I have come to realize is, I would rather be hurt by walking in truth, than to be appeased with a bunch of lies.

I discovered that my world was full of illusions. Once I began to see clearly through my version of what I thought was my reality, I began to question every single thing and person pertaining to my life and society in general that did not sit right within my spirit. What I saw was depressing. I saw a boat load of followers. Lies that were spread as truth. Hypocrisy in our government leaders. Fake people pretending to be real. You name it, I saw it. It was as if a foggy film from cataracts had been removed from my eyes and things were as clear as a sunny day. The scary part was that it was not what my natural eyes saw, it was the insight of what my

7 EMBRACE

spiritual eyes could see.

I became very depressed, some days barely getting out of bed. There were lots and lots of tears that I shed. I would have these dark moments for a few months, then I would come out feeling a little better, to only experience it all over again after a short period of relief. This went on several more times all within a 3 year span. The good thing was, each dark time was not as intense as the previous episodes.

However, each dark time exposed more and more of the people I was around and the things that were taking place in our society. I really cannot explain it with words, but it is a "knowing" that comes from deep within. Oftentimes, I can see things beyond what appears to the natural eye. It is not scary but it simply brings spiritual awareness to my common sense.

With every depressive experience, layers of my old self were being shed and eventually died off. A transformation was happening and I was learning to embrace this new person that was emerging out of the layers of death taking place within.

I could not explain it to anyone where they would fully comprehend it correctly. My friend Toshia was the only person at the time who "got it" completely. The reason she understood my dilemma was because her deceased mother had experienced some of the same things that I was sharing. She said her mother felt the same way and experienced similar emotional and mental pain. No one in her environment could quite understand exactly what she was dealing with and as a result she was sort of an outcast in her family.

However, her mother continued to live in her truth whether people understood her or not. She embraced the new self and was at peace with herself and her life. She no longer felt like she was in bondage to others thoughts and opinions that differed from hers.

Toshia not only listened to me, but she "heard" me and did not judge me for what and how I shared my experience and feelings. I took a different approach and chose not to share my experience with family. Instead, I researched and found others online that were going through very similar experiences that I was going through.

This was not the ordinary depression we hear about from medical doctors. Of course it had very similar physical symptoms like being lethargic, sadness, crying, anger, fear, and withdrawal. But I believe there was still something about this that was different from ordinary depression. One major thing that I noticed was that each time it would lift, I emerged stronger and better than when I was triggered and went down. It was as if layers of past pains and hurts were being destroyed and removed from my life. The new and improved me was emerging.

Similar to the story of the mythical Phoenix rising from the ashes. "As legend goes, when the Phoenix resurrects from the flames, she is more beautiful than before" ~Danielle LaPorte.

I considered going to a traditional therapist because I felt that maybe, just maybe, I was having some sort of breakdown because I have a family history with mental illness. When I would reach out and leave messages to make an appointment with therapists that I felt led to contact, it never failed, I would not get a return call back, EVER. Because my attempts failed more than once, I took that as a sign to not try to force myself to get therapy.

7 EMBRACE

As I researched this situation on my own, I stumbled upon some information that fit my description to a tee. I eventually found other people who had experienced this phenomenon as well. Some "experts" call it The Dark Night of the Soul. This is not a label that medical Doctor's use when making their diagnoses.

This was a spiritual journey and transformation. It has no association directly with "religious dogma" nor mental health issues. In fact, people from all walks of life with different faiths, or no faith at all have gone through the Dark Night of the soul and all remained mentally intact taking no medication during the experience.

A quick and easy definition of this phenomenon is: The dark night of the soul is a stage in personal development, when a person undergoes a difficult and significant transition to a deeper perception of life and their place in it. This enhanced awareness is accompanied by a painful shedding of previous conceptual frameworks such as an identity, relationship, career, habit or belief system that previously allowed them to construct meaning in their life.

For me, it seemed like I was in a meaningless universe, unable to bear going through the motions, having no sense of direction and feeling like I had lost all hope.

They say that The Dark Night of the Soul can be triggered by the tragedy of death, disasters that you can no longer explain, or a collapse in the framework of the life you once created in your mind. All of these episodes can spin you into this dark unexplainable space. My experience began in October 2017.

All I know is that my life changed almost one year exactly after Audrey passed, and it has never been the same since. I cannot even phantom going back to how things "used" to be. The dynamics have changed with my family, my marriage, my career, and even some of my beliefs pertaining to my Christian upbringing. I am very clear that I still choose to believe the core principles of Christianity one being, Jesus is the son of God and my savior.

This journey sparked something in me. It emerged a woman that had been suppressed and trapped by upbringing and societal expectations. I realized that I was not living in my truth. I was not being 100% authentic and this disturbed me greatly. I felt like a complete hypocrite not only in my environment but more importantly towards my own self. I could no longer live this way.

One of the first things I did towards my liberation to becoming confident and free was going skydiving. I was prepared emotionally, mentally, and spiritually to die if I did not land safely back on the ground.

Only for a couple of brief moments did I feel fear. The first time was when I was filling out all of the paperwork releasing the skydive company of any liability in the event of injury or death. The next wave of fear came when I was at the edge of the door of the plane about to jump. I seriously questioned my sanity as I peered down and could only see the greenery below. Once I got past the fears that were trying to make me turn back, I was not nervous at all. We were three miles up in the air and I was about to jump, I was ready.

The moment came, and the tandem instructor literally pushed me out of the door, there was no turning back now. The first few seconds, we dropped so fast that I could not hear my own screams. The wind was so fierce and strong that my face felt like someone had grabbed each side of my

7 EMBRACE

cheeks and was pulling them toward the back of my head. After a few seconds of free falling, the first chute was released. This chute would stabilize and slow down our drop. After a little time went by, the second chute was released and from that point on, it was an easy, quiet and tranquil glide down to the ground.

As I soared through the air, I felt so light and free. It was like I had released a ton of bricks off of my shoulders. A little weight of my former life had been destroyed by jumping out of that plane that day. I felt liberated. I felt like superwoman. If I could literally jump out of a plane, what else in life should I fear, I asked myself? People were the number one thought that came to mind. I feared people concerning their thoughts, ideas, opinions and judgements about me. It no longer made sense to me why I should even care what anybody felt about me, my life, or my decisions.

When we finally landed on the ground, I noticed my adrenaline was at 100%. My heart was beating so fast as if I had just ran a marathon full speed. I could barely stand up.

From that day forward, I have been actively taking steps day by day to become more and more confident and free. I was not the same person that initially went up in the sky. A new fearless me had emerged.

Daily, I am learning to be more authentic and live in my truth. I no longer feel bad for saying no to things that are not aligned with me or with where I am going. I am continuing to shed dead weight from things that are a burden to me. I am letting go of people that are no longer in alignment with my new path. I am embracing and loving myself first. I am healing and becoming whole in order to attract others that are whole.

LIVE CONFIDENT AND FREE

All of my issues of abandonment, rejection, low self-esteem, low self-worth, anxiety and fears that I struggled with daily, are healing and being released. I only surround myself with people who are leveling me up. Those that challenge me, correct me, and those that want to see me succeed are the only ones on my priority list of people.

I continue to study and research to improve my self-development. I meditate and pray for my spiritual health. I hang out in nature, and spend time with a few animals to balance my mental health. I exercise and do adventurous activities to improve my mental and my physical health. I experience different cultures and food locally and through travel to expand my world views. I rely on prayer, discernment, and intuition to stabilize my emotional health. As you can see, maintaining an overall balance in my life is what I strive to do as I continue to grow and move forward.

To become confident and free, I am not suggesting that you have to skydive or experience the Dark Night of the Soul to begin your spiritual journey. I think that it only takes keeping an open mind to all possibilities, experiences, and opportunities that may come your way. Be intentional on your journey. Ask God, and your angels for guidance and protection. Look for resources that will help you find the things and people that will bring out the best in you and add balance to your life.

Spend time trying new things outside of your norm. Discover new interests and activities that you can add to your own personal repertoire. When you begin to be intentional and focus on yourself, you will be amazed at what you will discover.

7 EMBRACE

BE CONFIDENT AND FREE: RISE ABOVE SELF DOUBT

Negative thinking can no longer reside with you on your journey to becoming confident and free. This does not mean that negative situations or thoughts will not arise in your life, because they will. It is up to you to recognize and be intentional when combating negative thoughts with positive thoughts, forgiveness, gentleness and kindness towards self.

It is very easy to be hard on yourself because that is a toxic pattern we have become accustomed to. Although the toxicity is familiar, it no longer has a home with you. You have evicted toxic behaviors from your life. You have made the decision to evict toxic people from your space. What this means is that you are now protecting your sacred space.

Anything or anybody that is not a good fit in a positive way must be removed or at minimum, have limited access to you. If it is not leveling you up to be a greater version of yourself, or respecting your new focus, it is no longer welcome. To be clear, this does not mean you have to isolate or cut people off (unless you need to), but you can set healthy boundaries and be firm in sticking to those boundaries.

Again, this is about creating healthy boundaries to protect your sacred space in mind, body, and soul. Continue to practice daily affirmations, meditations, prayer, walks in nature, and participate in activities that will challenge your creativity. Become aware of your surroundings, your environment, your thoughts, and the company that you keep. This will keep you grounded and centered.

BONUS

Celebrate The New You
BE CONFIDENT AND FREE BY TURNING YOUR TEARS INTO SMILES

You may have cried many days and many nights. Tears are merely a purging process. There is a need for the human body to release through emotions or reflexively. There may even be dry tears that cannot be shown or expressed at all. Whether the release of tears comes from a place of sadness and hurt, or happiness and excitement, celebrate the new person that is coming forth. Although I did not fully understand what was happening to me, I celebrated each time I let go of a part of my past that was hindering me from living my best life.

For me, during 2017 up to 2020, my tears were mainly from a place of sadness and grief. I was mourning back to back the deaths of people that I loved, but at the same time and probably more so than the grief of death, I was mourning the death of my former self and the life that I once knew. I literally experienced the death of my old self. I buried old beliefs, old ways of thinking, old patterns and behaviors. A part of me that had been suppressed began to come up and out. A new and different me began to emerge.

I found a new strength, a new courage, scales began to fall from my eyes, where I once was blind, I could now see with a new pair of spiritually enhanced eyes.

Along with this new found self, there also came with it, a lot of heartache and pain. I was not the only one that was being affected by this change within me. My career was affected, my marriage was affected, and relationships with friends were affected. I had to let go of people and things that no longer aligned with my new purpose. It had to go if it no longer served my highest good.

There was a lack of understanding from people on the outside looking in. I even had a hard time understanding everything. When I tried to explain what I was going through, I was only met with blank stares or the question of "what can I do for you to make it better?" There was nothing anyone could do. There were no answers. It was a part of the process and the journey. I quickly learned that I had to walk this journey alone. I had to learn to surrender, trust the process and let things be as they were. This is not to say that fear did not appear, it did, many times, but I could not let fear paralyze me.

Nowadays, I am more aware and in-tuned to my feelings. I recognize when self-sabotage tries to emerge. This usually happens when I become fearful and unsure of why things are happening in a certain manner or I will focus on the future with a bunch of "what ifs". By doing this, it causes me to not live in the present moment of right now. Trying to be in control does not work in this unique lifestyle.

A lot of my days are lonely, even if I am around oth-

BONUS: CELEBRATE THE NEW YOU

ers. However, although I get lonely, I accept that being lonely actually does not make me feel as sad as it used to. Basically, I am finally confident and free to be myself. This has outweighed the lonely days that come my way.

On some days I take field trips. These field trips consist of long drives to different attractions such as parks, museums, other cities, or recreational activities. Some are day trips. Some are overnight.

One trip in particular that helped change my perspective on life was a 5 day cruise to the Bahamas that I took for my 48th birthday, solo. I have travelled alone many times, but those trips were typically for business conferences or seminars. This trip was different.

I am naturally quiet and usually uncomfortable in crowds of people that I do not know. On this cruise, would I talk to anyone? Would anyone approach and talk to me? Would I still participate in the activities that the ship offered? I did not have the crutch of familiar friends or family to lean on.

Once again, fear came over me. But this time, instead of allowing the fear to cripple me, I faced it head on. I forced myself to step out of my comfort zone, put on a confident and free demeanor and carry on as if I was not the least bit bothered.

Several of those days on the ship, consisted of a lot of quiet time of self-reflection, past and present. I prayed, meditated, exercised and chose healthier food. I also made sure to get plenty of rest. There were times that I would go out and get involved in the ship activities. I went on a couple of fun excursions. I shopped, explored, and ate local Bahamian food.

LIVE CONFIDENT AND FREE

There were a few things I learned that week:

1. I have faced death a few times in my life and made it through. If I no longer fear death, why should I fear people, places or other things outside of my comfort zone? My biggest fear now is not living my life to the fullest before I depart this earthly body! I will no longer make apologies for how I want to live out the rest of my life. If my life choices happen to not align with societal standards or upbringing, oh well. This does not mean I am living reckless and on the edge. But taking risks is a part of life and I no longer want to live under the conditions of "what if".
2. I learned that life truly is what you make it. We create our own realities by the beliefs and standards that we live by. If you are the type of person that firmly believes that listening and believing everything the news, government, or even spiritual teachers tell you, this journey will be hard for you. It takes a very intentional approach to boldly ask questions on things that do not make sense deep within our gut. It takes courage to go left, even though you are more at peace going in that direction, everyone else may be going right. They may tell you that you are crazy or weird for going left.

These were just a few steps that I took towards becoming Confident and Free. By taking the first steps towards this new life, my tears began turning into smiles. A weight was gradually being lifted. My attitude turned into focusing on myself by loving myself, forgiving myself and accepting myself.

BONUS: CELEBRATE THE NEW YOU

To some it probably seemed very selfish of me to take this approach and in reality it was. But I had neglected Erica for far too long. It was now time for me to focus on myself. It was time for me to focus on my healing in every area of my life, mind, body, and soul; physically, mentally, emotionally, and spiritually.

Of course this was and still is a process in my journey. There are days that I am still crying, but the smiles come right after the purging. I have accepted that this is a part of the process.

After skydiving and my solo Bahamas trip experience, of course I faced some criticism. I was called crazy and a lunatic. I was asked repeatedly, why in the world would I jump out of a perfectly good airplane or why would I go that far on a trip by myself with all the stuff going on in the world? My answer was always the same, "why not?"

I was accused of having a midlife crisis when I got my first tattoo at 47. Two years later, I had my lip pierced. A good friend who somewhat understood my journey, asked me why my old ass waited to do all of this. All I could do was laugh and not perceive the question negatively. I responded with, "When I was younger I wanted to do many things outside of my "normal" environment, but they were frowned upon".

I was always taught it was a sin to put marks on your body in the form of tattoos. Piercings, aside from the ears, were for the weirdos or devil worshippers. Skydiving was for crazy white people. Although I have always been different in my thought process, I conformed to how my environment viewed things opposed to being my true self.

Another side eye I received from certain people was

when I travelled to Thailand in 2019. The flight was 24 hours long, with a few layovers. Although I was travelling with a group, I did not meet up with them until three flights later when I arrived in Japan. Therefore, on the first leg I flew 14 hours on a jumbo jet. I was alone on a plane full of foreigners that did not look like me, and you know what? It did not bother me one bit. I was not intimidated by potential language barriers or navigational issues once I landed on foreign grounds.

It was at that moment that I laid aside my American ways and expectations. I simply went with the flow, living in the moment. By doing this, my stress levels were replaced with peace. Any anxiety or fear that I had, was replaced with excitement and an open mind. Now, I do not care what people think or say about me.

Finally, I feel free to be me!

I am not afraid to do things alone. This journey to become Confident and Free forced me to be with myself to learn who I am. It has confirmed that not everyone I know can go where I am going. It is not to say I want to be alone, but if life leads me on that path, I think I could handle it much better these days with dignity and grace.

I honestly do not believe this walk will always be a lonely one. Because we are energetic beings, we will attract what we are. I think as my energy continues to change in a more positive way, I will begin to attract other people who are in alignment and on the same wavelength of energy as me.

Before, I loved to have company, but now, I am learning to not be codependent on anyone. The point is, there is a big difference with being lonely and being alone. A lot of

BONUS: CELEBRATE THE NEW YOU

relationships are centered on, codependency under the guise of love, friendship, or family closeness.

Sometimes in life we may have to go to many destinations alone. I realized this when witnessing my sister, my uncle, and a pet pass away. Death is one journey that everyone must go alone. Yes, you may be surrounded by loved ones on your dying bed and they will probably even hold your hand and talk to you. But one thing our loved ones cannot do for us or anyone else that is dying, is cross to the other side with a physical human companion.

While living, we should be perfectly okay with being in our own company, whether by choice or even when others are not available to accompany us.

While we are still living, we can change our perspective on how we view our lives and life overall. If we focus on the positives and let them outweigh the negatives, then we could truly live life with a smile through any tears that may arise.

We should celebrate this new life regardless of our experiences. Whether the experiences were good, bad, or indifferent, they helped shape and mold our character. Embrace every step in your journey. There is a purpose and destiny attached to them.

BE CONFIDENT AND FREE:
TURN DREAMS INTO REALITY

My prayer and desire is that you have received inspiration, encouragement, and motivation to get out there and LIVE! The phrase "we only live once" has since been reversed to "no, you only die once, but you live everyday". That is so very true. We have our birth date and our death date but what is going on with that dash in the middle is what really matters as long as we are still breathing. Therefore because you are still breathing, it is high time that you step out and live it up.

Now keep in mind, everyone's idea of living will be different and whatever your idea of living is, it is not up to me or anyone else to judge it. You will have to live with your own consequences or convictions. Only you can decide and envision what you would like your destiny to look like.

Whatever your idea of living is totally and completely up to you and you should not feel worry or guilt based merely on someone else's opinion of how they "think" you should be living. Now keep in mind, if your choices are destructive and harmful to yourself or others, then it is okay for loved ones to intervene. If not, then other people have to learn how to mind their own business and focus on their own life path and leave that person in the hands of the creator.

Whatever you choose to do, there will always be consequences, good or bad. My mom gave me some sound advice when I was around sixteen years old. Me and a friend of mine thought we would have some fun and agitate my mom a little bit. We brought up the subject of sex and birth control and why parents should be perfectly fine with their teens participating in both.

Mom told me and the friend that she would never condone having sex before marriage or to take birth control as a teenager. Those were her personal beliefs and convictions. Of course today, there are many other parents that would not have agreed with this so-called, outdated philosophy. However, my mom stated that if I chose to go that route of being sexually active and potentially getting pregnant she

BONUS: CELEBRATE THE NEW YOU

said with firmness and conviction, and I quote: "Make sure you can suffer the consequences of the choices that you make" and she left it at that for me to ponder and decide on what I was going to do according to my knowledge of right and wrong.

I never forgot those words. I live by them to this day. There have been plenty of choices that I have made that I suffered painful consequences. There were also choices that I have made that were great with great consequences as a result. In life, we will all make good and bad choices and for the most part, we will survive the bad choices. Some of those bad choices may come with devastating outcomes that will haunt us for years. Hopefully by facing our issues, healing, and learning valuable lessons from the bad choices, good choices will follow.

I think lessons learned are a natural part of life and growth to become a better you. If there were no mistakes to be made, we would be considered perfect, and last I checked, there is no perfect person on this planet.

With that being said, whatever your dreams or desires are, go after them with courage. Sometimes you will succeed and at other times you will fail, miserably. The key is to not beat yourself up if you make a mistake or fail. Failures are only lessons that need to be learned.

I was talking to a friend one day who had a very hard and abusive life living with a drug addicted and alcoholic father. He experienced his father beating his mother and verbally abusing them. Living with the fear of the father's anger and wrath was a daily thing.

This childhood trauma followed my friend into his adult years. He made many, many bad decisions. He became a part of a gang, had several close encounters with death, the police, etc. He was basically wildin' out, doing drugs and having many sexual encounters. One day he finally got caught and had an encounter with the law on two different occasions that landed him in jail both times, with the second arrest potentially earning him many years in prison.

These two events had a major impact on his life in a positive way. I told him, sometimes we may have to encounter tough situations to make positive life changes. Instead of beating himself up about his seemingly "bad choices", I flipped the perspective on him and asked him what lessons did he learn that changed his life. As he began to list the lessons, I told him if he had not gone through what he went through, he would not be a testimony to others who need to hear his story of abuse, living a hard and wild life to get to the road of redemption that he is now walking on. He is happier, more at peace, and loving his new life.

When he viewed it from that perspective, he could only agree that the experiences had greater good even though they came out of a horrible situation. He is now living his best life sharing his story in ministry, while inspiring and impacting lives one beautiful soul at a time.

As you continue moving forward on your journey and path in life, embrace, love, and celebrate the new you that is coming forth and emerging out of the, just like the Phoenix Rising.

Are You Ready to live Confident and Free?

After going over the 7 powerful steps to becoming confident and free, now you must ask yourself are you ready to step out there and do the work.

BONUS: CELEBRATE THE NEW YOU

You may not ever experience what I have experienced with the Dark Night of the Soul or any other of the personal things that I experienced. You may not ever experience any triggers that point out emotional issues, mental or emotional abuse of abandonment, rejection, fear, or anxiety. However, overall self-improvement and self-development is never a bad thing to tackle when working towards being Confident and Free. Like the Phoenix, eventually the real, authentic you will arise out of the flames and ashes.

The key to becoming confident and free is to simply make a decision and vow to yourself that you will be intentional and strive everyday to become the best version of yourself possible. No, you will never arrive at perfection, but improving imperfection is the goal here.

Do not look at your past as failures or mistakes. Look at the past as lessons for your growth to be a better you. If you have been living with guilt or in bondage from past choices or mistakes, it is time to be let it go and once and for all, forgive yourself!

I used to be hard on myself when I felt that I made bad decisions with relationships or with friendships in general. As I grew, I chose to view mistakes as necessary lessons that I needed to learn. I try to no longer judge or criticize myself harshly no matter how bad I was hurt, disappointed, or used.

Each lesson made me into the woman I am today. The confident and free spirit who had suppressed her real authentic self to fit into "normal society". Now I question what is normal? There's a quote by Charles Addams that I absolutely love. "Normal is an illusion. What is normal for a spider is chaos for a fly".

LIVE CONFIDENT AND FREE

What is your normal and what is your chaos? I guarantee yours will be different from others you compare it to. The key here is to not try and align yourself with someone else. You have to be who YOU are and no one else. Being your individual authentic self is what we should strive for.

If you are quirky and weird, smart, intellectual, silly or comedic, etc. embrace yourself fully. Love every bit of yourself genuinely. When you begin to do this, you will notice that you will start attracting people who are like minded and embracing their true self also. Others will be drawn to your individual style and personality.

I was so shocked, when I started walking in my truth and building my confidence, I was attracting all sorts of people both male and female. I had people telling me they were intrigued by my lifestyle, my mysteriousness (whatever that is), my personality, the way my eyes looked, etc. I had never in my life been told such things before. My past compliments were based on my physical appearance only.

The only rational conclusion that I could come up with was that my soul and spirit were illuminating.

I once heard a YouTube influencer say, "You don't have to be the sexiest or prettiest one in the room, but your confidence and individual style is what is attractive." He was giving an example of a young lady at a party whose looks would be considered about a seven. Although she was amongst a whole bunch of tens, she stood out because she did not look like the normal stereotypical 10 female with long hair (hair extensions mainly) and surgical bodies. She was an individual who wore her hair in its natural state and she had an eccentric style of dress. Best of all, she walked with confidence and that made her super attractive.

BONUS: CELEBRATE THE NEW YOU

You don't have to be eccentric to stand out, but being your true authentic self is what is important and will shine bright. People can see through fakeness if they are aware and paying attention. Sadly, our society has totally embraced fakeness, lies over truth, and mask wearers.

However, no matter how much society has embraced and accepted this, there is still a genuine interest in the mystery of authenticity.

People actually admire others who are not afraid to be different from the norm. They envy others who go against the grain and refuse to be a follower. Even if people talk about you, I am almost convinced that the haters secretly wish they could have enough courage to be their true self also. They can see the freedom that comes with this. They can see the confidence that one carries. They secretly desire to be confident and free also.

Since you have gotten this far in this book lets me know you are ready to live a life of confidence and freedom. Right now is the greatest moment in your life to manifest your dreams into reality. You no longer have to sit on the sidelines watching others live out their dreams wishing you could do the same.

You have the power to turn your dreams into reality. All it takes is making that one decision and then committing to do the work. It took the death of my loved ones for me to get triggered and decide to live my best and more authentic life. There was tremendous pain that came up but I knew I wanted to live differently than I had been living.

I encourage you to go skydiving or travel if that is on your bucket list. Go create that song album you have always desired to do. Start that business you have been afraid to put out there. Go write the book you have always thought about writing. (Honestly, it took me eight years to write this book. It was an idea that I had outlined years ago but I never put any action behind it. At the time, I was not even sure what it all meant when I wrote down the ideas, but as you can see, the vision became clear in due time.)

All it took was a few traumatic events that I had not healed from, to trigger me in such a way that I never would have imagined. At the time, I didn't think I would ever get past the pain and recover.

I knew I had a purpose and a destiny to fulfill. Because my entire life has been impacted and changed, I have people (my tribe) eager to receive my talents and gifts through me walking in my purpose. Lives are waiting in the que to be touched.

But God, in his infinite supply of grace, wisdom, and mercy allowed me to have a conversation with three trusted friends about my idea of starting a life coaching business centered on becoming Confident and Free. A fire was lit under me to move forward. I was challenged by one friend to set a deadline in completing this book you are now reading. I was held accountable until the book was completed.

Another friend constantly asked how my book was coming along each time we spoke. To be honest, some days my friends got on my nerves asking me how the book was coming along and how I would make the life coaching segment become a reality. But in all honesty, I was really irritated with myself on those days that I was slacking. Their words of conviction got the best of me and only propelled me to take inspired action.

I truly thank God for these people. They have been a

BONUS: CELEBRATE THE NEW YOU

tremendous support and they truly desire to see me succeed. Remember earlier in the book when I told you it is imperative to surround yourself with a supportive environment? It's because you will need it.

I do not know what it will take for you to go after your dreams or to live your life to the fullest, but I hope this book can be a catalyst, to light a fire under your behind to go for it, whatever "it" may be.

Surround yourself with supportive people who are not afraid to tell you when you are wrong. Get people in your corner who will hold you to a higher standard of accountability. Find the kind of people who will stay on you to get things done. Yes, they may irritate you, get on your nerves, and possibly use a few choice words some days, but that is their job to keep you moving forward even when you do not feel like it.

There may be days when you want to give up but if you keep your vision top of mind, you can and will succeed in what you have set out to do. You may have to shed a few tears and feel some pain, but your weeping will turn into joy. I love the quote "I never knew a storm that didn't pass". Storms are not exempt from your life's journey. They will soon pass and the sun will shine again. If you see a rainbow, that is even better. It symbolizes that good fortune, peace and serenity is headed your way.

You cannot allow your passion to die if you encounter a few obstacles in the road. I can attest that it is never a smooth and straight lined ride. There will be twists and turns, hills and valleys, but you will overcome them by staying focused on the ultimate goal. You have to live your life with the expectation that things will ultimately work out for your good. When you raise your vibrational frequency to being a better you, you cannot help but to attract good things. The good will always supersede any unforeseen force that will try to abort the mission with negative vibes that you may encounter along the way.

After you have accomplished some or a lot of what you desire to accomplish, there is one thing that I ask of you, and that is to pay it forward. Do not hold back from lending a supportive hand to another individual that wants to be released from the bondage of society and live a more confident and free life as well.

Pass this book along to any soul that may need to be encouraged, motivated, or in need of some life coaching to help push them into their destiny and purpose. Or perhaps you are the one that needs a push. Do not hesitate to reach out to me for coaching help. Rest assured that this is a safe and nonjudgmental environment.

We cannot get arrogant and think we are too far ahead of others who are not as far along on their journey as we are, and ignore or turn our backs on them. We all started out crawling before we walked.

We also cannot get upset with those who refuse to improve. If they are stuck with living in a less than stellar or in a mediocre life, that is their choice. The beauty of life is that we all have free will and choice. Everyone has to walk their own path their own way, whether we agree with it or not.

With that being said, go and make a conscious decision to become an even better YOU!!!

Cheers to living a Confident and Free Life!

ABOUT THE AUTHOR

Erica Aker is a 30-year veteran in the beauty industry. Having listened, counseled, and offered different perspectives and advice to thousands of women in what seemed like hopeless situations, Erica now uses that experience and training by shifting her business from standing behind the styling chair, primarily focusing on the external appearance of women, to now, a certified Transformation Life Coach who focuses on the internal woman that is typically suppressed and hiding mainly due to…FEAR.

After having coached many beauty professionals and clients on business and personal matters, Erica has now expanded outside of the beauty industry and stepped into her passion of coaching the everyday woman (and a few smart men) in the business of LIVING!

OTHER BOOKS BY ERICA AKER:

- *How to Create and Build a Successful Beauty Business* available on Amazon.com (Hardback)
- *How to Build Momentum in Your Beauty Business: A Quick Start Guide to building a Business You Absolutely Love, Win Loyal Clients, and Grow Your Income Fast* (Ebook)
- *3 Massive Mistakes Beauty Pros Make That Kill Their Income and How You Can Avoid Them* (Ebook)
- *Money Makeover, It's Your Time* (Ebook)

To contact the author, go to:

Website: www.confidentandfree.com
Email: erica@confidentandfree.com
www.facebook.com/erica.hugheyaker
www.facebook.com/confidentandfree
www.instagram.com/EricaAker
www.instagram.com/_confidentandfree
www.youtube.com/confidentandfree
www.linkedin.com/in/EricaAker/
www.pinterest.com/EricaAker
Twitter: @EricaAker

www.ingramcontent.com/pod-product-compliance
Lightning Source LLC
LaVergne TN
LVHW041708060526
838201LV00043B/631